The Road To Joyful Living!

Whatever you do in life you will do it better by being cheerful and kind to others. Make a smile your calling card, a helping hand your stock in trade and laugh your way to a better you!

Cover by SelfPubCovers.com/JohnBellArt/JTR

i

NOVELS BY JOSEPH T.RIACH

Too Early For A Glass Of Wine?

and

* Coming Soon – New Mystery Thriller *

SUCCESSFUL LIVING

The Secret World Of Self-Employment

Mastering The Art Of Making Money

Self-Improvement Should Be Fun!

Winning Big In Life And Business

The Simplest Sales Strategy

The Road To Joyful Living!

Because I Feel Like It!

Yes You Can!

Available in Paperback and Ebook at Amazon (.com and .co.uk), Barnes and Noble and other leading book stores. Visit Tom at www.tomriach.com

THE ROAD TO JOYFUL LIVING!

Joseph T.Riach

ISBN : 979-8511092300

Joseph T.Riach

The Road To Joyful Living!

CONTENTS

1 – Expectation
in which you preview the route ahead

2 – Education
in which you visit your roots

3 – Imagination
in which you are encouraged to dream

4 – Motivation
in which you strengthen your resolve

5 – Realisation
in which you uncover your inner self

6 – Cooperation
in which you share the joy of service

7 – Valuation
in which you examine your true worth

8 – Determination
in which you challenge yourself

9 – Valediction
in which this road ends and your journey begins

The Road To Joyful Living! is my rewrite and update of Self-Improvement Should Be Fun, first published in November 2017. With love and thanks for the tireless support and encouragement of Erna.

The Road To Joyful Living!

PART 1

Expectation

in which you preview the route ahead

Joseph T.Riach

ABOUT THE AUTHOR

Joseph Tom Riach was born and brought up in the Scottish city of Aberdeen and educated at its famous Grammar School. So too was Lord Byron in a previous era. A both precocious and introvert child, Tom was an obsessive footballer and outdoor pursuits enthusiast. He once set fire to the family home while lighting a camp fire in the sitting room. He also liked to write.

In young adult life Tom's independent spirit and drive saw him quickly set up in business on his own account. As a serial entrepreneur, he established, acquired and operated several small businesses.

He learned that the success of his enterprises was primarily dependent on effective promotion and sales of the goods and services he provided. Tom soon came to the conclusion that employing good life skills and promoting himself as a trusted partner to potential clients was the most effective and enjoyable way of getting ahead. What he learned to practice is the simple psychology of being happy at what you do and sharing that happiness with and helping others.

As a result of his significant business success, he was engaged to enlighten the marketing and sales teams of other companies with regard to his success strategies. What he taught was how to excel in business through being a 'good person', employing relationship building techniques and helping people improve their situations.

His unique approach meant that he had unwittingly become a life coach to industry!

It became somewhat inevitable therefore that Tom would in due course turn to writing about this central aspect of his success in life strategy. This book is it.

In a modern world awash with self-styled internet gurus, lifestyle coaches and 'how to' merchants he stands out as one who has actually been there, seen it and done it. As regards the t-shirt – he probably manufactured it! When he speaks, it pays to listen.

This is your opportunity. Don't waste it!

ABOUT THIS BOOK

These writings originated from my work coaching aspiring entrepreneurs and sales people in the 'soft selling' and relationship building techniques which I developed and successfully practiced throughout my business life. However, it became apparent that my methods centred on what were nothing more than practicing good life skills, being happy and helping others. My philosophies and practices can, I believe, benefit all people in all walks of life by encouraging you to :

Concentrate only on the positives in people

See the humour and joy in every situation

Find ways to help others

At the beginning of my career I set out with the aim of creating material wealth and becoming successful. Although I worked tirelessly I achieved little of either. However, over time, through experience and with the counsel of those older and far wiser than myself, I learned that the sure route to real spiritual wealth, lay not in working on the commercial aspects of life but was to be found in concentrating all of my efforts in helping others. So that is what I did. I focused purely on helping others. It is from that strategy that success flowed.

The question arose as to how many others could I, should I help? Answer – as many as possible. But is that hundreds, thousands or even millions? I was perplexed. Then I remembered a conversation I had had with a friend many years previously. The friend had been dismissive of my pursuit of wealth and its trappings, expressing instead their desire to save endangered species, the tiger in particular. In response to this I had posed the question, "How many?" My point being that to save the beautiful creatures would take the very money which my friend so despised … and lots of it! My friend's response 'though was simple and clear - "I want to save them all."

That became my starting point too. To this day it remains my goal … I want to *help everyone!*

This is the most important personal development principle which I have to pass on to you.

Whatever you want from life, the best way to get it is to focus your energy in helping others.

• *If you want higher self-esteem then find ways to boost someone else's self-esteem.*

• *If you want to raise your positive spirit then assist someone else to raise theirs.*

• *If you want more happiness in life the smartest way to get it is to help someone else achieve it.*

When you give generously of your time and effort in these ways then, in due course, you will discover as if by magic that the biggest beneficiary of your efforts is .. you! You'll become spiritually rich, relaxed, confident and inwardly calm. One fully in harmony with your inner self.

~

Each time I cast my mind to the exotic kaleidoscope of experiences with which my life is liberally peppered, I am constantly and pleasantly surprised to be reminded that even the most bizarre events of my existence are what primed me for, and propelled me to become the man I am. The key of course being that I was neither deterred nor hindered by obstacles and unfortunate events nor got carried away with the successes. I learned from them all and determinedly used the experiences as stepping stones to future glories.

I have used some of these personal stories and anecdotes from time to time in this book, both for the purpose of illustrating certain points and to entertain you. However improbable (and life does tend to throw up the sublime and ridiculous does it not)? they all happened. Author's licence permits me small embellishments at times and timelines are occasionally altered. The consequence remains 'though that I have learned a universe of valuable lessons from the experiences inherent in them.

As a result of which I practice today what I consider to be the simple truths of life. I consider myself immensely privileged to have lived through these hills and dales of life's bumpy crust and that I am permitted to share them with you here.

~

Throughout this volume you will encounter some repetition of certain texts and passages. I've included these by choice, it is entirely intentional and for the following reasons :

Repetition is a powerful way to learn. In the first book of my *'Successful Living and Personal Achievement'* series, *'Mastering the Art of Making Money'*, I have written a chapter entitled *'Repetition, Repetition, Repetition'* which addresses this topic. In that text I stress the importance of using repetition to enforce messages and cement them in your mind. In repeating some passages within my works I am simply practicing what I preach!

I also consider certain messages within this publication to be so profound as to merit repetition. Not that profound equates to complex, quite the opposite. In fact the closer you get to truth, the simpler lessons become. Life is actually incredibly simple. It is the complications which humans create that blind people to the simple truths of life which are far and away the most meaningful. They are thus basic and essential learning. No apologies for hammering home these points with repetition.

Lastly, my writing covers the four crucial aspects of your being :

Mental : *Physical* : *Spiritual* and *Material wealth*.

I firmly believe in and promote the concept that these aspects of life are inextricably linked one to the other. Therefore many of the lessons to be learned appropriate to one element are equally applicable to the others. Sections in this work dealing with one aspect of life sometimes repeat guidance given in other sections dealing with other life aspects. This repetition also occurs between my various books published.

For instance, in writing *'Mastering the Art of Making Money'*, I make reference to the need to practice good life skills and to self-promote effectively. In *'The Simplest Sales Strategy'* I stress the point that good sales skills are no more than good life skills and vice versa. Then here in *'The Road To Joyful Living'* I emphasise the point that personal development requires acquiring and practicing good life skills and nurturing self-awareness and confidence.

The need to learn and practice good life skills appropriate to both your inner self and your outer being is common to all areas of your existence ... material, mind, physical and spiritual. It is the understanding and implementation of this over-riding principle which you must take on board in order to realise improvement in all areas of your life. This is my core belief and the central theme of all my writing and teaching, both business and personal.

My hope therefore is that the content of this book will be an inspiration and a constant source of positive reference to you throughout your life. What you learn could also alter the course of other lives which you touch ... and it could be you who gives this priceless gift to them!

Joseph Tom Riach

Joseph T.Riach

PROLOGUE

Charlie Chaplin and Adolf Hitler were born within a few days of each other in April 1889. They shared far more than just a birth date. Each possessed an obsessive personality, extraordinary work rate and a generally tyrannical attitude to those around them. What differentiated the two men was not their birth dates, neither their personality nor their talents. The big difference between them lay in how they used their respective talents.

One chose a life of power, corruption, murder, mayhem and destruction, all in the pursuit of world domination. The other chose to become a clown and entertainer and to bring laughter to millions. While it is easy to acknowledge the power of the gun and of brutality one should never under-estimate the power of comedy.

In fact, when comparing the lives of the two men one could justifiably say that Chaplin had the last laugh. His most successful film, '*The Great Dictator*', was, after all, a satirical political parody of fascism, antisemitism, the Nazis and Hitler. Is it not true that laughter will always prevail over adversity? Is humour not the last bastion, the final refuge of man's inherent spirit? For even in the most desperate of situations, even at the death, does man not often raise his middle digit in defiance at the Grim Reaper and find a suitably humourous line with which to blunt his scythe?

Chaplin himself purportedly said, in response to the "May the lord have mercy on your soul" prayer of the priest attending his final hours, "Why not? It belongs to him anyway!"

The killer final words of all time surely came from the great

11

Voltaire who, when asked on his death bed to forswear Satan said, "This is no time to make new enemies!"

Yet the most significant point to all of this is that both of these giants of the arts, Voltaire and Chaplin, each blessed with a talent beyond the norm used that talent in positive ways which enriched their own spirit and brought enlightenment and joy to the world. They demonstrated by example that a dedicated approach of being constructive and well humoured in their pursuit of excellence need not be ruthlessly destructive.

It's an easy choice in life to do nothing, to act negatively, to blame others and indeed to be cowardly, aggressive and murderous. There are many of the last-inclined abroad in the world today, behaving despicably and trumpeting the same tired old line 'that a higher power instructed them' to perpetrate their ghastly crimes. These criminals would have put to death those who laugh at their idiotic doctrine. Why? Because they fear the power of comedy and humour.

They realise that as long as man can laugh in the face of adversity and can confront their attempts at tyranny with wit and satire then, just like Adolf Hitler all those years before them, they are doomed to failure. The power of comedy far surpasses and outlives the power of the aggressive bully. Laughter will always drown out the rhetoric of tyrants. No-one should ever doubt the profound influence of the comic on society, culture and indeed history.

Hitler boasted of a Third Reich which would 'last one thousand years', but in the end little Charlie Chaplin was the one who achieved world domination.

So make good humour central to your personality, make a smile your calling card, spread joy and fun where-ever you go ... and laugh your way to a better, richer life!

Joseph T.Riach

The Road To Joyful Living!

PART 2

Education

in which you visit your roots

Joseph T.Riach

Chapter 1

WHAT IS SELF IMPROVEMENT?

What is self-improvement? What does it mean? What is it that you're hoping to achieve by improving yourself? You'd better know the answers to those questions before reading further because self-improvement can mean a lot of different things to different people. Anyway, do you need improving? If so why and in what ways? Let's find out.

The term 'self-improvement' broadly refers to the act of undertaking to work on the improvement of your knowledge, status or character through your own efforts. It can help you to make positive changes in all aspects of your life and can be applied to your life in general or to specific areas of your life, your being, activities and personality. For example :

Physical health and well-being

Your physical and mental well-being is the foundation on which all other aspects of your life are based. Attending to these should always be of primary concern. Engaging in healthy physical activities, regular exercise and sport along with adopting healthy eating habits and nutritional diets are areas that many of you will want to improve on.

Personal skills and abilities

Developing abilities and talents for your own benefit can not only be a source of personal satisfaction but can lead to greater work and professional opportunities and also help you to understand your limitations in these areas so that you can work on making improvements. You can also be motivated to learn new skills or take up new hobbies, past-times or interests which themselves will increase your prospects of living a fuller, more rewarding life.

Social and relationship management

Enhancing interpersonal relationships through identifying how your own psyche works and in how you interact with others enables you to make positive changes which will impact on your social behaviour and how positively others view you.

Overall personal improvement

Your primary aim in self-improving should be that of teaching yourself to think and to see yourself in such a way that you have the confidence to take control of every aspect of your life .

Then, be it physical health and well-being, personal skills, relationship issues or whatever, you will have the ability to handle them all! You will develop the inner strength and character to allow you to rise to any challenge in life and achieve any objective which you set yourself.

It's a fact you see, that even the most outwardly, apparently confident of you suffer to some degree from self doubt. Every person on the planet does. Everyone experiences those dark inner voices which prevent you from realising your full potential.

What many of the most super confident individuals have done is re-programmed their inner beings and trained themselves to overcome anxieties so induced; they can present a face which is unfazed by other people, events and situations. In fact, the most successful 'improvers' will have totally eradicated from their mind, and especially from their deepest subconscious, all reference to any negative thoughts. Such people have learned to convert negative mental energy into mind forces that inspire and empower and which help them defeat those destructive, deep-seated thoughts which typically hold you back from believing in yourself.

Love and kindness

The last, but critically important aspect of self-improvement, is what I term *'Love and Kindness'*. In other words, how good are you to your fellow man? What value do you add to the lives of others?

Make no mistake, the more that you give to other people in this world, be it material, physical or spiritual, then the more life will pay you back. The more reward that you receive in this way, then the more you will come to experience deep gratitude for life's simple blessings and from that you will grow as a person. The greatest beneficiary of your love and kindness will be yourself.

More expressly your view of your own worth will soar in direct unison with the value that others place on you. Now that's self-improvement!

POWER POINT - *"Live life, laugh and love!"*

In the following pages you will find some reference to psychology but not a great deal. You are not about to be bombarded with complex psycho-babble or overly intellectual analysis of the subject of self-improvement. Although I do suggest that psychology is a subject with which you should familiarise yourself.

What you will find is a simple 'route map' to a better understanding of yourself and what makes you tick in a collection of practical recommendations and guidelines. These are easy and straightforward ways to go about bettering yourself and how you feel about yourself, bettering who you are and what you do. All are practices, thoughts and methods of behaving which you can enact in small ways and on a daily basis – and starting right now!

Aim to be the best that you can be … but remember, there is no 'finished product' with regard to self-improvement. It's a lifetime work in progress.

Chapter 2

THE GREEN GRASS OF HOME

In the classic "Green Green Grass of Home" hit song, the subject sings longingly of returning to his childhood home on his first visit since leaving in his youth. He dreams fondly of his parents being there to greet him as he steps down from the train and of his beloved Mary running to join them. All around is welcome and peace and every one of his family and friends come to be there, smiling sweetly and with arms reaching out to embrace him. The singer easily recalls features of the place such as the old oak tree that he used to play on and poignantly reflects that it's good to touch the green green grass of home. And why not? He's talking of returning to his roots.

You all have roots. For some of you, deeper than others. They exist for all of you. No matter how far from them you are or how long it is since you returned to the place of your beginnings, you will experience to some degree a yearning to revisit them. It's sometimes referred to as home-sickness. It's a condition which affects some of you more often and more strongly than others but you all come from somewhere and at some point will reflect on the fact. These thoughts of 'home' are most often positive ones as in the song. But not always.

There are those of you who may have deliberately cut yourself off from your roots. That is you have consciously decided to have nothing to do with the place of your birth and/or the people and situations in it. You feel completely disassociated from your beginnings, disinterested perhaps. You have effectively enacted a divorce from them and all that they represent. You may feel that you have good reason for feeling this way.

Whether this extreme of emotion applies to you or not, it's reasonably certain that in almost every case, touching base with your origins from time to time is both a healthy and a necessary thing to do. If you are set on self-improvement, bettering yourself or simply learning more about what makes you function as a person, then a visit to your personal 'green green grass of home' is pretty much an essential start point.

If your memories are somewhat less than the brilliant, emerald green chord struck in the song and you are in some respects disenchanted with the experiences of your childhood, then you are still recommended to revisit those places and times in order to confront the unpleasant memories, deal with them and put them to rest. Then you can move on with your life and to being the person you long to be.

Of course there may be those who have embroidered in their mind an altogether much sunnier tapestry of their birth place and time than was the actual case and for them a reality check may do no harm either. After all, a balanced life requires a balanced view of who you are and who you want to be. That means understanding and taking on board who you were too!

It's well to bear in mind that, just as there is a tendency among some to believe that the grass is always greener on the other side of the hill, so too is there a certain pessimism in assuming that the other side will always be a bleaker place. Grim perceptions of who you are and why you are the way that you are, based on distant childhood recollections, are as likely to be exaggerated as are memories of the *'permanent sunshine holiday'* type. Either way a visit to your roots will serve you well.

It will take you to the time, people and places which you inhabited in your earliest, formative and most impressionable years. It's here that you discover the origins of your deepest, often loudest 'inner voices'. You know the ones, those instructions which still to this day control many of your basic impulses. The *"No elbows on the table"* and *"Don't speak 'til your spoken to"* type of commands issued by parents and teachers ... and which you still instinctively react to or enact. Plus the more sinister *"No-one wants to hear what you have to say"* type statements etched into your subconscious.

I was in my mid twenties when in the midst of an argument I blurted instinctively and without reason, "Why is everyone allowed an opinion except me!" There followed a momentary silence before my fellow squabbler queried, "Who says you're not entitled to an opinion?" That floored me.

I later gave much thought to that exchange and came to realise that I harboured a deep feeling that my opinions were in some way unworthy. Further soul searching revealed that these thoughts had originated from my parenting in early childhood and had become rooted in my subconscious persona. I had the assertion hammered into me so many times that I really did believe that my opinions did not count!

Fortunately for me and my future development as a mature and self-assured adult, that particular argumentative exchange disclosed not only the rogue implant referred to but it also set me on the road to self-discovery and the unraveling of my whole personality and behavioural patterns. It remains a lifetime work in progress.

But the single most important lesson I have derived from it is that, in order to understand others you must first understand yourself. Once you've got a handle on what makes you tick then you are far better placed to work out other people's behaviour. Only then can you truly empathise with them and come to know how to relate to them in the ways that are most beneficial to your own personal development. Because never forget the crucial message, and you will read this repeatedly throughout these pages - *how you perceive yourself is how others will perceive you.*

If you are indeed that guy who does believes that the grass is greener on the other side of the hill, who constantly prospects about how much better things are for someone else, somewhere else, then others will see you as being constantly dis-satisfied. But when you are, and see yourself as being happy and contented with your lot in life, then that's how people will see you too.

Be warned, it will always be easy for you to lose concentration on the task in hand (improving your self) and slip into negative thoughts and ways. When you do there is a remedy you must employ. It is quite simple. You should first actively concentrate on reminding yourself of the many joys in your life, the simple things which you often take for granted.

Take some quiet time to yourself, somewhere with peace and solitude. Close your eyes and picture your family and loved ones and the joyful way they respond to your presence. Remember the good health which they and yourself enjoy, the fresh food you eat and the clean air you breathe. Be thankful for the roof over your heads and the prosperity, great or small, you create and share. Starting now, practice this as a daily exercise. You will find reflection like this to be inwardly rewarding, peaceful and rejuvenating.

While feeling thus rejuvenated, take time to mentally delve into your childhood. Dig up memories. Humourous or traumatic moments seem to recall best. So try to trigger memories of the *'dad falling into the stream'* or *'you gashing your knee and going to hospital'* type of event. Significant and trivial, all count. Your early schooldays and as far before that as you can get to are the best place to commence your search. As the images of those far off days come back to you (and you will get better at recalling them the more you work at it), figure out how they relate to who you are, what you are and how you are today.

Does memory of your green green grass of home inspire safe, loving feelings and sweet scents or does it stir in your being emotions of fear and trepidation?

You will soon arrive at the realisation that improving yourself today starts with finding, and coming to terms with, who you were yesterday!

Joseph T.Riach

Chapter 3

JOSEPH'S COAT OF MANY COLOURS

I was born in Aberdeen. It was memorable for the fact that my mum was in Cambridge at the time! But in time she forgave me that inconvenience and knitted for me from left over pieces of wool my first bathing costume. It was emerald green, banana yellow and held up by suspenders with large gold buttons. I debuted as the only four year old transgender canary at the local pool! The other kids could barely conceal their mirth so didn't try ... and chucked me into the deep end for an extra laugh.

The lifeguard of the day was equipped with a twelve foot long pole with a hook on the end to ensnare the swimwear of those in difficulty. But when he tried to fish me out of the water with it, my wool costume simply unraveled. Another bather, witness to the unfolding fiasco, eventually dragged me unconscious to the side of the pool and applied resuscitation.

When I came to my mother was so relieved that she smacked me round the ear as punishment for ruining my swimming costume. Then she sent me to nursery school wearing a smock she'd made from old curtains.

The standard issue smock bought from the posh department store in town and worn by every child except me was a light beige in colour. My one featured green foliage, massive pink flowers and frills! That and the fact that I was a Joseph (a name considered 'sissy' by the other kids in that time, place, culture) guaranteed continuous hilarity for all ... and a lions' den of misery for me.

But the time came when an enactment from the bible story of 'Joseph and His Coat of Many Colours' would be performed by the class. I had the name and I had the coat. I was a natural for the part! A star was born. Following that success never again would I be ridiculed and my mother's reputation as a bohemian fashionista of remnant clothing burgeoned.

From those experiences I grew in stature and learned to resolutely fend for myself, to be self-confident and humourously self-deprecating. There are those who say I take criticism badly but I say, "What the heck do they know?!"

To this day I stand up for myself and tend to support any who I see being taken advantage of. I treat others respectfully and expect no less in return. Life can deal an apparently bum hand ... canary swim suits and flower emblazoned smocks ... yet it's how you play the hand that counts.

You can choose to fold and accept an existence of moribund mediocrity ... Or you can go all in and seize the prize of a glittering life.

Like me, you can be Joseph and his coat of many colours. Try it for size!

The Road To Joyful Living!

PART 3

Imagination

in which you are encouraged to dream

Joseph T.Riach

Chapter 4

THE PROOF OF WHAT WE DREAM

As a child I was berated for day-dreaming. It was considered to be a sign of an idle mind.

As a lad I dreamed of becoming a footballer –

At age seventeen I played my first game as a professional.

As a young man I dreamed of working for myself –

At age twenty-three I set up in my first business.

As a businessman I dreamed of great achievement –

By age forty I owned several businesses which gave employment to more than seventy people.

As an entrepreneur I dreamed of international success –

By age forty-five I had completed assignments in a dozen different countries.

As a traveller and free spirit I dreamed of life in a warm climate and continental culture –

At age fifty I left Britain to live in France.

As an ex-pat living abroad I dreamed of schooling visiting guests in life and business skills –

At age fifty-two I started my 'Wake Up Leisure and Learning Breaks.' (note 1)

As a life and business coach I dreamed of authoring my own

work –

At age fifty-four I wrote my first book and sold it by mail order.

As a writer I dreamed of writing a series of *'Successful Living and Personal Achievement'* instructional books based on my knowledge and experience -

The first of these - 'Mastering the Art of Making Money' - was published in February 2016.

As an author I dreamed of writing a best-selling novel -

My first novel, 'Too Early For A Glass Of Wine?' was published in November 2019. It sells successfully all around the world.

Yet … As a child I was berated for day-dreaming!

POWER POINT - *"You become what you dream. So dream well!"*

Note 1. Wake Up Leisure and Learning Breaks – Personal Mentoring and Business Guidance courses conducted by the author in the south of Portugal. Information at https://www.tomriach.com/wakeup

Note 2. 'Mastering the Art of Making Money', 'Too Early For A Glass Of Wine?' and all of Joseph T.Riach's books and novels are available from the online Amazon book store, Barnes and Noble and other leading book suppliers.

Chapter 5

IMAGINE THE IMPOSSIBLE

The thing in life which I most love is my work ... and even more so a challenge! Were anyone to have the temerity to suggest to me that some proposed venture or project I was embarking upon was impossible then they're best advised to do so from a safe distance and wearing full combat gear!

Working on an 'impossible' undertaking is, you see, everything to me. So much so that the actual end game, the achievement of a successful conclusion, leaves me feeling empty.

Hence the need in my life to embark quickly on to the next project and then the next and the next and so on. My imagination will not, cannot stop. This is why I and all those like me never stop 'dreaming and scheming'. How do you retire an active imagination? Why would you stop doing that thing in life which you most enjoy?

To those not of this disposition, I say *"Dare to imagine the impossible!"* Why not? What is there to lose? Only a humdrum existance devoid of adventure. What I refer to as 'the sleep of the living dead'. Such people go around in what amounts to a daze, unaware of real life or of living it in the here and now. It's akin to being devoid of all senses. Yet, without sensuality there is no joy! Only the darkness of a cold non-existence.

Don't fall under the spell of the living dead as personified daily by the media, bleak soaps and reality TV. Break free, think for yourself. Embark on a life full and vital. Embrace the simple pleasures – sunshine, fresh air and helping others. Be your best self at all times, living every day as if it were your last.

POWER POINT - *"Dare to day-dream - imagine the impossible!"*

Chapter 6

DIES HE SLOWLY

He came from I know not where but there was he before me, a towering giant of a life lived well. I inquired of him as to how he filled his days given that his every need was met. Piercing eyes - was there a hint of amusement there? - and a calm air of self-assurance greeted my query. His vigourous response, also a question, lanced back.

"Do I look alive?"

He most certainly did.

"And do I look happy?"

Yes to that too.

"Then there is your answer – I live happily."

POWER POINT - *"The secret of life is ... to live happily!"*

To live happily he explained meant doing the things which he most enjoyed, 'fulfilling his wants' as he put it. Top of his list was his work. He continued to be fully active in all of his many enterprises and in a hands-on manner, "I'm no back seat boss!" he proclaimed.

Second on his list was helping others less fortunate than himself. Not with pity nor with hand outs but by supplying knowledge, opportunity and resources with which the deprived could, if they chose, create their own improved circumstances.

"The under-privileged must be driven by the fortunate few to help themselves, otherwise they simply slip back into their unfortunate existence," was his measured summary.

"Those two activities," he added, "My work and my philanthropy, occupy fifty per cent of my waking time."

This revelation was followed by a deliberately manufactured pause, fully intended to prompt the follow up question pertaining to his use of the other, unexplained fifty per cent. So the question was dutifully asked.

"Ah that time .... ," and now he was reflective, profound. He drew a purposeful breathe, "That time is for .... dreaming!"

At this moment he pre-empted the next query betrayed by my involuntarily flashed, quizzical glance.

"Yes, I did say dreaming. Dreams you know are the spring of my ambition, yes I continue to have things which I want to achieve. Dreams have been the source of all my inspiration. They are everything to me, they are my very life blood. Know you not that dies he slowly who does not dream?"

POWER POINT - *"Dreams are the spring of ambition and the source of inspiration. Dies he slowly who does not dream."*

"Without dreams we wither and fade away because bereft of imagination we are nothing ... not me and neither you."

Then he was gone.

Had he been himself but a dream? Not so. For there where he had purposefully placed it and caressing my minds eye was the dream of a glorious dawn bathing my being in the towering realisation of a life lived happily.

The Road To Joyful Living!

PART 4

Motivation

in which you strengthen your resolve

Joseph T.Riach

Chapter 7

FIT TO BE A BETTER YOU

I have always been one of those lucky people who can eat as much of whatever I want yet stay as slim as a pencil. Of course I make my own 'luck' too. As a kid I was the exact opposite of today's desk-shackled computer generation. I was forever on the move. I ran everywhere. I'd run the mile to school and back each day, play endless football matches in the school yard, climb and hike in the mountains and swim in the sea. Then there were physical training periods at school, games days, the athletics club and gymnastics, more football, rugby, cross country runs and the swimming and life saving clubs. Life was a blur of constant action.

My first real organised training sessions started with the school rugby team when I was twelve years old then picked up pace at fourteen when I started to play for my first youth football club. Since then, give or take the odd break, I have trained every day of my life. At my peak I was training rigourously for two hours twice per day and was as fit as any Olympic athlete. Today things have slowed somewhat but I still exercise most days.

As a life-long business entrepreneur were I to be asked how I define myself, I'd answer, "As an athlete first and a businessman second." You see, like many other aspiring athletes, when success and the prospect of a sustainable income-producing career in sport didn't materialise, I redirected my energy into business. The business arena is a tough one. A competitive, even cut-throat environment, demanding effort and dedication. Only the most resolute prevail. It thus goes a long way to satisfying the competitive instincts of a frustrated sports-person.

Whether you're going to be in business ... or if you're not going to be in business ... it's as well to be physically fit. Fitness will sharpen your performance all round, raise your awareness and intensify your thought process.

Of course you all know of, or have encountered, people prominent in society who are grossly overweight or heavy smokers or who never exercise – who are anything but fit. This would suggest that physical fitness is not a necessary prerequisite to doing well in life. To those who are of that view I'd simply say, "Imagine what such people could have achieved had they been fit too!"

I have written elsewhere that, *"There is nothing you do in life that you won't do better through reading a book."* I'd add to that that there is nothing that you do in life which you won't do better by being physically fit.

POWER POINT - *"There is nothing that you do in life which you won't do better by being physically fit."*

I read recently of a multi-million dollar research programme having been completed by doctors at a leading university in which they concluded that physical exercise improves brain function. My reaction was one of amusement. The (famous) phrase, "I could have told them that!" came to my mind. Indeed I could have told them that (and at considerably less expense)! because I know from my own experience that my physical exercise not only keeps my body in shape, it keeps my mind toned too. The two work in tandem, they feed each other.

Constant training, day in and day out takes will and determination. That comes from the mind. But the exercise itself sends oxygen, nutrients and cleansing agents around all of the body, including the brain, and thus keeps it sharp and in good working order. So physical training is brain training and vice versa. It's win-win!

POWER POINT - *"When you exercise your body, you exercise your mind and vice versa. It's win-win!"*

In addition I actively practice brain exercises. Simple things like running through my multiplication tables first thing in the morning when I awaken to the more complex research and authorship projects I undertake. Any work involving active brain usage is in fact brain exercise. Writing this material is one .....

As success is something that we all strive for, whether in small ways or as in major achievements, it's important to recognise that successful people generally employ a very simple plan of action which they repeat over and over. In fact, simple activities carried out repetitively and well are what mount up to great achievements.

POWER POINT - *"Simple activities carried out repetitively and well are what mount up to great achievements."*

Daily exercise is itself a simple, repetitive act. It instils confidence and self belief as well as invigourating the body and mind. It should be an important part of your life success plan.

Are you fit to be a better you?

~

The Atlantic hammers with relentless anger into Portugal's west coast ... and creates at Nazaré the fiercest surf on the planet. Small wonder that crowds surge there to gasp at the spectacle. When winter storms add their weight, the seething walls of foam taller than tower blocks prove an irresistible magnet to the fearless daredevils of extreme surfing.

It was here in November 2017 that Brazilian surfer Rodrigo Koxa set the official world record for the largest wave ever surfed, by successfully riding a 24.38 metre (80 foot) high giant. But American Garret McNamara surfed a monster as ferocious as any force on earth and reliably estimated at an almost unbelievable 100 foot in height in 2013!

Can you imagine how the experience, the thrill must have felt for him? Probably not. But I ask the question because both McNamara and Koxa, not to mention the many other extreme surfers present on these awe-inducing occasions, and all the members of their support teams had imagined it beforehand … over and over again.

You see they didn't just turn up at the beach on spec with an old board and wet-suit and pop into the water for an al fresco splash. They had first as youngsters dreamed of surfing the waves, then had practiced, trained and prepared for many years, building strength and experience, acquiring knowledge and technique. So, by the time that they entered the water they were as well equipped as any person could be to confront the challenge awaiting them.

Of course there was still risk. That same morning of McNamara's one hundred foot blast, Brazilian professional Maya Gabeira had to be resuscitated on the beach after being knocked unconscious under an 80 foot cascade. She was fortunate both to be rescued and to survive with just a broken ankle. It took her years to overcome the physical and mental scars of the experience. But, in January of 2018, she returned to face her Nazaré nemesis. She successfully surfed a 70 foot (20.7 m) giant and set a new female world record. McNamara himself suffered a dislocated shoulder and broken arm in a near death 'wipeout' off the California coast in 2016.

But without risk there would be no challenge. And to be up for the challenge you must be prepared. Anything less is just plain foolhardy. So these are the lessons to be learned by all regardless of how big or small is your horizon in life or business. Dream success, imagine it, plan for it, be ready ... then when the moment comes to confront your own personal breaker have the courage and commitment to ride it for all you're worth.

Rise to life's challenge, take on your personal world's biggest wave.

~

Huddled in the soaking cold of the trench, the Corporal grabbed the letters thrust at him by the mail runner and immediately ripped them open.

The first was from his mother. It spoke of home and longing to see him return safely.

The second was from his sweetheart. It spoke of love and desire and a wish to hold him in her arms.

The third was from a complete stranger. It told how the writer and his family were homeless and without food and begged for help.

The Corporal quickly scribbled his replies on the backs of the originals, for time was short.

To his mother he wrote - "It is hard but I am well. Thank you for all that you have done for me. I hope you will be proud of me."

To his sweetheart he wrote - "I love you and hope to be with you soon. But if things go badly you must promise to carry on and enjoy a full life."

And in the third reply …. in the third reply he wrote - "I am sorry to hear of your plight. Enclosed is my last pay cheque. I hope it helps."

Then he went 'over the top'.

The Corporal you see, although young and under stress – or perhaps because of it - realised some things very fundamental to being.

His mother and his home were of a past that could never return.

His sweetheart and her love were of a future that might never be.

But the war and the plight of the strangers were *in the here and now and he could do something about each of them*. So he did. He did what he had to do and he did the best that he could do.

So honour those that selflessly give of their best in all times and honour yourself by being the best that you can be each and every day. Live life in the present.

POWER POINT - *"Live life in the present and, whatever the circumstance, always be the very best that you can be."*

~

The bullet that killed me was travelling at one thousand feet per second. It was fired from a Smith and Wesson .45 ACP by a shallow youth much given to using the word 'respect'. Yet he himself possessed neither self-respect nor a microfibre of understanding of the meaning of the word.

In the improbable event that he survived to mid age then he

might have grown to know of the fragility and preciousness of life. He might have learned to empathise. If he did, he might have wondered about the man whose life he stole all those years before. Who was he? What was he like?

He'd have discovered when researching that I, like himself, had been a wild lad given to some violence. But also that I'd been brought up to honour my elders, authority and the rights of others. So my natural rebelliousness was tempered by respect.

He'd have learned that my uncompromising and dispassionate approach to life and business had brought me success but that I only experienced joy and fulfillment once I understood and practiced compassion and forgiveness.

He might have come to see that the bullet discharged from his handgun on my fatal day, had it been human and possessing of integrity and empathy, would have declined the uneven contest with my brittle skull. It would at least have preferred a face to face confrontation with an opponent of equal magnitude and stature.

Better still it may have chosen to stay in the chamber.

In so doing the bullet that killed me would have chosen honour and respect.

That's my choice too.

What's yours?

Joseph T.Riach

Chapter 8

KNOW YOUR ANGELS

Do you believe in angels? I do. Not the cherub with large wings floating in the air kind but those fellow humans who protect and support us; those who arrive out of the blue just when we are most in need. On some occasions they appear not even as humans …..

"It was a daft thing to be doing but when in ones teens and seeking the quickest route home in the early hours of the morning following a night on the tiles, walking on the railway line seemed like a perfectly reasonable action. But suddenly I was shocked out of my homeward nonchalance by a huge German shepherd dog clearly intent on doing me serious harm. It charged towards me as if from hell, teeth bared and barking viciously. Instinctively I threw myself to the side just in time to avoid the onrushing hound .... and also the inter-city overnight express which sped by from the opposite direction!

So lost in my thoughts had I been that I had not heard the train arrive. Had it not been for the perfectly timed 'attack' of the crazed dog, I wouldn't have heard it depart either! Picking myself up from the undergrowth at the track side, I prepared to defend myself from the expected onslaught of the wild beast. None came. In fact, there was no sign of the animal anywhere. Had it been struck by the train? No, there was no evidence of that. So shaken and thoroughly awake I made my way home.

Nearing my apartment I bumped into my flatmate, also

returning to our pad in the early hours. He greeted me with a slightly puzzled look and asked, "Where did you find that scraggy brute?" Turning in the direction of his gaze, I saw padding along behind me the mystery, and frighteningly unpleasant looking, alsatian which had saved my life! It stayed on my doorstep, fed and watered by me, for three days and three nights. On my return home from work on the third day the dog had gone. On the doorstep where it had stayed keeping watch over me lay ... a single white feather."

As human beings it is inevitable that we will experience ups and downs in our lives, good days and bad days. We use our experience, knowledge and wit to minimise misfortune but we will still fail at times. That's why it is essential to be not only firm and resolute in our behaviour, but to be kind and considerate too. Because when you do show compassion for others and act on it you are being their angel at the time when they need one. And your angelic act will be returned to you when comes your hour of need, not always directly from the person you aided but often from an entirely different direction.

POWER POINT - *"A kindness given will always be returned when you most need it 'though often from a different source than to where originally gifted."*

It is important therefore to be on the look out for your angels arriving. You may not recognise them at first as they come in many guises. If you miss them, through misplaced pride, ignorance or cynicism then your chance for redemption may be gone.

Stay alert. Your angel may appear as the friend or relative you've neglected these many years or as the guy from across the road you've always (probably for no real reason) disliked and who you assumed disliked you. Your angel will often materialise as a total stranger or one whose appearance or character at first didn't appeal to you. Or they may come to you as an employer, workmate, neighbour, acquaintance or business colleague.

Your angel may even come in the form of a scraggy hound from hell! But be assured - your angel(s) *will* come.

When they do, welcome them, encourage and nurture them. Surround yourself with them. There are few things more important than to know your angels.

POWER POINT - *"There are few things in life more important than to know your angels."*

~

The businessman stuffed a couple of large denomination notes into the hand held out by the homeless wanderer and then gifted him all of his loose change too. All that is save for one coin which he carried with him at all times. It was a coin very special to and cherished by the man of fortune. It was his permanent reminder of a time past when he too had been destitute .....

"It was Christmas eve. Homeless, cold and hungry, Tom thrust his palms deep into thread-bare pockets in a fruitless attempt to find some warmth. One freezing hand settled on the only two coins he possessed. He rubbed the coins thoughtfully and then, summoning up his resolve, went to the nearby phone booth and, inserting one of the coins, dialled the familiar number. His adult daughter's cheerful welcome raised his spirits. Unaware of his plight she engaged in playful seasonal banter until Tom, swallowing his final vestiges of poverty-shredded pride, did the hardest thing he had ever done in his life. He asked his daughter for money. But she easily responded to his plea for help, some cash would be wired to arrive quickly.

The task he had been dreading having been accomplished, Tom turned his attention to how in the meantime he would keep himself fed. Soon he made his way to a local bakery and sought out the owner. To the baker he made the proposal that he would, entirely free of charge, create an attractive advert for the bakery and have it placed prominently on a leading website with a considerable local following. Tom would need to first sample the baker's wares in order to establish the quality of the goods to be promoted! An understanding nod and grin from the baker accompanied the box of pies and rolls which he handed to Tom as he slapped his shoulder and wished him festive cheer.

Next Tom crossed the road to another local business where he was familiar with the owner. To this entrepreneur Tom proposed that he would, again entirely free of charge, build a new direct marketing programme guaranteed to increase his business substantially. To do this Tom would require to work overnight on the businessman's office computer when the office was empty and the computers not otherwise in use. Tom started work that very night.

Tom now had a small sum of money to tide him over, food enough to feed himself for a week and a roof over his head at nights for a month or more. Most importantly he had given himself a life-line, a glimmer of hope, something to build on. He didn't waste the opportunity.

Within a year the marketing programme devised and implemented by Tom for the local business had increased that entrepreneur's client base two fold. The bakery prospered and continued to reward Tom with free bread and pastries for many years. In return for her 'life-saving investment', Tom's daughter benefited to the tune of many thousands of dollars.

In adversity Tom had learned humility and his dire situation had driven him to find imaginative solutions to his plight. His fortune was restored but Tom would forever be a changed man."

The businessman pondered awhile on the memory of those dark days, sentimentally fingering his lucky coin saved from all those years ago. Then he wished the street dweller well and walked the short distance to the centre for homeless people. Once inside he discarded his warm jacket, rolled up his sleeves and enthusiastically made his way to the kitchen to commence serving Christmas dinners to the needy. He smiled inwardly. This was far and away his favourite part of Christmas!

POWER POINT - *"With humility comes compassion and inner joy."*

Joseph T.Riach

Chapter 9

THE END OF THE ROAD

S ir Harry Lauder was the renowned Scottish music hall and vaudeville singer and comedian during the early years of the twentieth century. He was famous for wearing extravagant full highland dress and carrying a gnarled cromach (walking stick) while performing; his appearance being almost a caricature which lent itself easily to some ridicule. But, as they say, all publicity is good publicity and his image, rich brogue, distinctive singing voice and repertoire of self-effacing tales of Scots' meanness turned him into a worldwide star. In fact, at the height of his fame, he was the highest paid entertainer in the world!

Not bad for an Edinburgh laddie, one of seven children of a master potter who died young leaving Harry's mother to fend for and bring up the family and necessitating young Harry (Henry was his real name) to start work at the age of just eleven years. He worked first in a flax mill and then for ten years as a coal miner before earning his first five shillings as a performer when he was persuaded at short notice to fill in for an inebriate indisposed singer in a local music hall. It wasn't quite a case of 'from there he never looked back', many hard years 'on the road' honing his skills and perfecting his act followed but by 1912, when he appeared top of the bill at the very first Royal Command Performance in front of King George V, Harry Lauder was a household name around the world. Nowhere was his international acclaim greater than in America.

To this day, many fine British performers aspire to 'make it big' in the USA - and fail! But Sir Harry was taken to heart by his American audiences who relished the nostalgia for the 'old country' and pathos inherent in his act. More than anything else, they saw in him a kindred spirit, a battler, a laddie from a poor family put out to work in a coal mine as a child yet who had overcome adversity and an under-privileged background to become the biggest star of variety theatre the world had ever seen!

Lauder's story is indeed one of inspiration. A lesson for all those who have ever aspired to better themselves. Proof, if proof be needed that, whoever you are, whatever your circumstance, it's always possible to drag yourself up from lowly status, reach for the stars and achieve the impossible.

POWER POINT - *"Whatever your situation it is always possible to pull yourself up, reach for the stars and achieve the impossible."*

Generations before Bob Dylan or the Beatles or others appeared on the scene performing material of their own composition, Sir Harry Lauder wrote all his own 'greatest hits'. He was the original singer/song-writer super star! Immortal numbers such as *"I Love A Lassie"*, *"Roamin' In The Gloamin' "* and *"A Wee Deoch-an-Doris"*, he both penned and performed. But his one song which perhaps best of all epitomises the man himself and his never-say-die spirit and with words that could have easily been purpose written for a modern day motivational speaker is :

> *Keep right on to the end of the road*
>
> *Keep right on to the end*
>
> *Though the way be long*
>
> *Let your heart beat strong*

Keep right on round the bend

Though you're tired and weary still journey on

Till you come to your happy abode

Where all you love and been dreaming of

Will be there at the end of the road.

Harry Lauder you see, understood better than most, that in life and business perseverance is everything.

Do you possess the iron will to keep right on to the end of the road?

Joseph T.Riach

The Road To Joyful Living!

PART 5

Realisation

in which you uncover your inner self

Chapter 10

THE REAL YOU?

In the first instance there is your spiritual self. This is your core inner being. It's who you are, it cannot be altered.

Then there is your subconscious mind. It controls all your involuntary physical and organ functions. More than that it is also the depository of knowledge and experiences of which you consciously remember nothing but which have been implanted there from birth. First by parents from early childhood and throughout, later by other agencies such as school, peer groups and society at large.

These deep subconscious memories cause you to act, speak and behave in completely involuntary ways over which you have no control.

Unless that is, you consciously work at reprogramming your subconscious to function differently!

It can be done. With hard work, belief and application, elements of your subconscious thoughts, beliefs, responses, words and behaviour can be altered.

Changes to your subconscious must be triggered from your conscious mind. That mind which is restless twenty-four/seven, planning, picturing, scheming and chattering ... and which turns those thoughts and images into the words with which you present yourself to the world.

Your words are the conduit between your thoughts and your

actions. You first imagine a scenario, then you articulate it (often write it down) and then you enact it.

So the natural elements of your being in sequence are :

* *Inner being, spirit*

* *Sub-conscious mind*

* *Conscious mind*

* *Words*

* *Actions*

I believe that you must understand these elements and how they function together from your inner spirit outwards, in order to grasp how you can live your life more fully and become a better person.

While the purpose of my teaching is to raise your awareness of these, it is equally to demonstrate how, by taking conscious control of and working on these processes, you can radically change the way you are, who you are.

The method is to do things in reverse. In other words you start by carrying out actions and work back to your inner being.

The key actions are always the same, and they are simple. You do things to make people happy and feel good about themselves.

POWER POINT - *"Make your purpose to do things to make people happy and feel good about themselves."*

Then you reverse the mind-to-word process. You use your words openly (repeating mantras and other information) to tell your conscious mind to instruct your sub-conscious as to what you've done, what you wish to do, who you are, how you feel and how to speak about it.

Your sub-conscious then absorbs and incorporates your instructions as being 'you'. In due course your 'involuntary personality' will speak and act as you have reprogrammed it to do.

Lastly and critically, your sub-conscious reports the changes to your inner spirit which rejoices at the nourishment and enrichment bestowed on it by your actions! You become a better person within your deepest being.

The single most significant factor which differentiates many very assured people from everyone else, but which is invisible to the casual observer, is that these super confident individuals have learned to use their subconscious brain power.

POWER POINT - *"Many very assured people have learned to consciously tap into and use the power of their subconscious."*

This allows them to appear to be more clever and able to cope with far more than other people when, in fact, they are no more clever or able than the next person.

Using the power of the subconscious is itself quite simple. Everyone does it at times but without realising it. For instance, you have certainly at some time experienced the answer to some question or point of contention suddenly 'coming to you' at a particular moment, perhaps days or even weeks after first trying to remember it. This is the result of your subconscious at work. Think also of how often you drive your car from A to B with no conscious effort, often unable to recall passing certain places yet perfectly able to hold a conversation or dwell on other thoughts while driving. This too is an example of the subconscious at work naturally.

Many self-assured people have realised not only that this immense power of the subconscious exists but also that it can be consciously harnessed and tapped in to. They deliberately – rather than leaving it to accident or chance – assign much work, resolving of situations and dealing with difficulties to their subconscious. As the subconscious can deal with an infinite number of complex calculations, memory searches and creative and reasoning tasks, and do so with no stress or apparent effort, this leaves the individual free to dwell on those matters requiring immediate conscious effort.

POWER POINT - *"Learning to use your subconscious brain power expands infinitely the volume of activity with which you can cope and your ability to reprogramme your core convictions."*

What's more, those who recognise and use their subconscious brainpower in this way programme their subconscious to produce results according to date and time parameters. Know what? - It always produces and on time!

Try it for yourself. Start with simple little memory tasks. Let's say for example that you know, but temporarily cannot recall, the name of the author of "The Man Who Mistook His Wife For A Hat" but want to recall the writer's name in order to impress your psychoanalyst as to your own sanity when next you visit him! Simply say to yourself out loud, "I will recall the name of that author before 3pm on Friday." Then forget about it and get on with your life. I can absolutely guarantee you that, at some time before your Friday 3pm consultation, your subconscious will come up with, "Oliver Sacks". It's an absolute dawdle for your subconscious to recall the name of the renowned neurologist, so keep working on similar simple memory tasks for starters in order to limber up.

Then build up to asking your subconscious to produce plans of action for more complex situations in your life or business. Give it a realistic time parameter – even your subconscious will struggle to produce a design for the next generation of deep space exploration craft in a week! Feed into your brain as much information as possible on the subject so that it has all the material needed to allow it to do the work. It can't produce the result without proper priming and without you having done the conscious homework. You should soon come to realise that the power of the subconscious is truly amazing and is without limit.

Armed with this knowledge you can begin to work on re-programming your subconscious with positive messages about who you are, your core convictions and how you intend to be. This is the deepest and most significant aspect of learning to use the power of your subconscious.

This power, remember, is not the exclusive preserve of confident people. Everyone possesses it. It is however the case that many very self-assured people have realised that this power exists and have then employed it in order to bolster their self-assurance!!

Thus they can deal with an infinite number of situations effectively while remaining calm, relaxed and at ease with life. Now here's a really important point. Being calm and relaxed and happy with your life equals being self-assured and confident. Only when in this state can you truly be the best you that you can be.

POWER POINT - *"Be the best you that you can be by being calm, relaxed and at ease with life."*

Employ the power of your subconscious to help you get there.

~

It is generally the case that whatever you do in life, be it a work, professional, personal or leisure related activity, you will do it better and enjoy it more if you are physically fit. When you are involved in physical fitness training as a daily and life-long action it is almost inevitable that you will become aware of the fact that while you are working to keep your body in shape you are also exercising your brain and invigourating your mind.

Constant, day in day out training takes will and determination, that comes from the mind. The exercise itself sends oxygen, nutrients and cleansing agents around all of the body, including the brain, thereby keeping it alert and in good working order. Physical fitness sharpens your performance all round, raises your awareness and intensifies your thought process – it's win-win!

So, is physical training the easy way to a healthy, worry free life? Well yes ... but not entirely. Because there is another very effective way which virtually guarantees that you will never again be ill nor require time off your work. This other way is called ... self-employment! It works like this :

After you become self-employed you soon discover that you can't afford financially to take time away from your enterprise ... time is money, your money! When you contract a heavy cold, flu, tummy bug or sore head you tend to work on through it. There just isn't the incentive to stay home as is often the case with paid employment which might pay you when you're off sick, has other people to cover for you and anyway, is not your business! As your own boss you over time just become used to working on through the discomfort.

Then a funny thing happens. You become aware that you are not experiencing the illnesses anyway. A time arrives when you realise that not only do you never suffer from any of the earlier-mentioned minor ailments but that you've never experienced any sickness at all. In fact you hear yourself saying to all and sundry, *"I never get ill."* And it's true, you don't!

What's going on? Simple answer - it's your subconscious mind at work (the same one you've kept healthy and alert with all that physical exercise)! You have primed it with your constantly repeated mantras or affirmations, first that, *"I can't afford to be ill"* and then that, *"I never am ill"* until' the instruction is so deep rooted in your subconscious mind as to be your actual state of being. In this case a state of being in which you never get ill.

That is why self-employed people are considerably less prone to illness and are party to significantly lower rates of illness-related time off work than their employed counterparts. They deep down believe they will never be ill therefore they never are!

So, in order to enjoy the easy way to a healthy worry free life … become self-employed!

Of course, there's a broader message here too. I am indeed a huge fan of self-employment. I have worked for myself for almost my entire working life. Apart from the greater financial opportunities it presents, it more importantly offers far greater scope in terms of personal freedom and having control over your own life. If you want to self-improve then becoming self-employed is not a bad idea.

However, whether self-employed or not, of greatest significance for self-improvement is for you to work at changing yourself through having a vision and reprogramming your subconscious accordingly. The way to do this is relatively simple but it takes application and determination.

You must make repeated positive affirmations of :

* Who you want to be

* What you want to be

* How you want to be

… and do so with conviction and perseverance until what you have told your subconscious is what you become. "I'm never ill," clearly proves the point - just ask any long term self-employed person! Remember that most of them did not consciously create their new reality. With them the change came about almost 'by accident' as a consequence of a life style need. By comparison, imagine the power when you tackle it as a conscious act!

First decide what you want, your vision, then you can start creating it. **You are no longer going to let the world create you, you are going to create your own world**.

These are the essential elements of positive affirmations :

* First consider who and what and how you want to be and be perceived as

* Frame short, sharp messages which express your desired changes

* Limit yourself to just three maximum – but concentrate on just one at any period in time

* Write them down and keep them displayed in constant view

* They must contain only positive words e.g. Not "I'm not ill" but "I am healthy!"

* Never ever use the negative of an expression nor negative words

* Affirmations must be in the present tense e.g. "I am happy

and confident!" You are experiencing the changes NOW!

    * They should be short not complicated. Only a few words as shown, no detailed or lengthy monologues.

    * Short rhymes or catchy jingles stay in the mind and work well. You'll find yourself reciting them constantly – that's what you want!

This is how you practice them :

    * Constant repetition (out loud is best) of each affirmation at least twenty times at any moment and at all times throughout your day

    * Do so at all times - First thing in morning, last thing at night, while jogging, exercising, showering, bathing, driving, taking a break, meditating, quiet moments – any time

    * Quiet times of solitude, peace and tranquility are best. Close eyes, breath deeply and slowly, visualise the reality and truth of your affirmation

    * State your affirmations with energy, intent and emphasis

And here are some simple examples :

    * I am healthy, happy and free

    * I am healthy and strong all day long

    * I am at the top of the hill (if running to get there) … or

    * I am the champion of … (enter whatever sport or pursuit)

    * I am caring, I am sharing, I am daring to be … (enter your intention)

- but in all instances visualise yourself as already there … already with the partner of your dreams, in the place of your dreams, performing the function, professional or leisure, of your dreams, behaving and believing as you dream of doing. In short, affirm that you are already living your dream!

Only you and you alone are responsible for your mindset. If your already installed ways of thinking are not serving you well then replace them with upbeat and positive beliefs which will create good energy in and around you. Then wonderful things can happen.

There really is no limit to the power of the subconscious and there's no instruction that it cannot take in and adapt to. It just takes determination and repetition on your part. When you find yourself stating as a fact or acting out automatically and without conscious thought, some belief, opinion, situation, action or emotion which you deliberately placed in your subconscious, then that is when you know that you have successfully reprogrammed it to represent you as the person you wish to be.

Start making the changes now, however small. Allow the new, fresh, joyous and happy to flood into your being.

Tell your subconscious that - *"Every day in every way I'm getting better and better."* And you will!

Chapter 11

GLUM AND HAPPY

Two brothers, Glum and Happy, were sent to a monastery school for a three year residential course of reflection, meditation and soul searching with an order of monks dedicated to silence and solitude. There they were confined to study in their spartan cells with neither outside contact nor conversation, other than for the one time at the end of each year when the Abbot would visit, inquire as to their progress and permit them a few words.

At the end of the first year the Abbot went to Happy's cell and asked if there was anything he wished to say.

"Oh yes!" said Happy enthusiastically, "I want to thank you for this marvellous opportunity and for all that I've learned so far from my time here."

The Abbot was well pleased with Happy. He then went to brother Glum to ask of him the same question. "This cell is cold and damp, my bed hard and my habit itches," was Glum's reply.

A second year passed and once again it was time for the Abbot to allow his novices a few words. He visited the brothers and asked them each the same question as the previous year. Happy told him with excitement about the books and manuscripts he had been reading, how stimulated he felt by the knowledge gleaned and the explanations and theories of the authors. He was looking forward with relish to showing the Abbot next year the thesis he was now working on. Glum complained that the food was rubbish.

Another year passed. The brothers' education was complete and they were released from their solitude and subjected to their final appraisal. Happy passed with flying colours. He did indeed spend many hours discussing his thesis with, and receiving the critique of, the Abbot. The Abbot for his part reported to the boys' father what a splendid pupil Happy had been. He was confident the boy would take his joy of life out to the world and be a valuable and popular member of society.

When asked by the father about his other son Glum, the Abbot simply replied, "All he ever does is complain!"

He then went on to discuss with the father how it is that people, all people, create their own reality in life, how they view life and how others see them. How what you see as the reality of life is down to your own perception of it. This had rarely been more clearly demonstrated than by Happy and Glum.

Both attended the same monastery, both were subject to the same regime, conditions and opportunities. How each perceived their situation was, however, quite different from the other.

Happy chose to perceive his situation as one of peace and opportunity, where he could learn and grow from his experience. Therefore others perceived him in that way too ... as a contented, ambitious and likeable lad destined to do great things in the world.

Glum, on the other hand, saw only gloom and doom. He perceived his life as that of a prisoner in a dark place. He was utterly disenchanted with his existence there and ensured by complaining that anyone he came in contact with shared his unhappiness. In this state he stagnated. There was no personal development. Because of that he was perceived as a miserable waster, unlikeable and one to be avoided.

What Glum, and all those like him, do not realise is that this perception of them by others is but a reflection of how they perceive themselves!

POWER POINT - *"How others perceive you is but a reflection of how you perceive yourself."*

Before others can see you as you wish to be seen, you must first ensure that you yourself embody the perception you want others to have of you. This will not be easy but it is simple to start and there are daily actions you can take in order to build your confidence.

First you must rid yourself completely of all negativity and negative influences.

Negativity is not what I am about, it is not what this book is about and it's not a subject I wish to write or speak about. I have absolutely no wish or desire to even mention the word!

But negativity and negative people do exist and for the purpose of making the comparison with positive energy and positive people and situations, it is necessary to refer to the word. Let's make such reference as minimal as possible though. Let's major on just the positive, optimistic and joyful. Let's get rid of negativity - and starting now!

The simple message regarding negativity, negative people and situations is that you must shut them out of your life. You must do this completely. Those negatives that are already in your life must get kicked out first.

Now this can sound tough to take on board because many of these negative influences may be friends or family. Outside agencies such as negative media or television (and a huge amount of what they purvey is negative) are easier to eliminate. Learning and exercising self-discipline can take care of those. Being ruthless, and that's what you have to be, with those closer to you will take greater resolve.

Yet who you surround yourself with is central to how you yourself will prosper in life. With something as critical as your very existence at stake you cannot afford to pussy foot around. You must be decisive. If you are not then these people will drain your positive energy relentlessly, enmesh you in their hopelessness and hang you out to dry like a wet rag alongside the tattered remnants of your hopes and aspirations. Don't let them!

Your responsibility to yourself and your glorious future must come first. That starts with eliminating all negativity and the people who spread it like the disease which it is. No exceptions.

POWER POINT - *"Be ruthless in kicking out all negative influences from your life."*

Don't be afraid to assert with simple clarity to all those around you, who you are and how you expect the ambience in which you live your life to be. All those unwilling or unable to enthusiastically provide you with the positive support and encouragement you need, you must leave behind. Your journey to a better you will not include them.

This action will, not entirely surprisingly, alienate you from many. Friends, relatives and colleagues thus dumped are not likely to be your greatest well-wishers. Some may even become quite hostile. They may wish you to fail and will spread doubt, ridicule and negative talk about you, who you are and what you are doing.

Such action of course is driven by their own insecurity. They don't wish to see someone else, especially a former 'acolyte of misery', accomplish things which they themselves lack the ambition or discipline to attempt. They'll try to sabotage your efforts.

Such malcontents, while unwittingly adept at dismantling their own lives through their warped and negative behaviour, need have no effect on yours. This for the very reason that you have shut them out, and done so completely.

However, the modern world in which we live is awash with negativity. It leaks from every news bulletin, TV soap opera and political propaganda. It is endemic in society generally and the people with whom you brush shoulders each day.

In order for you to rise above and repel this tsunami of bleak pessimism with which you are confronted and the hordes who spread it, you must ensure that *your positive conviction and certain vision is so firmly cemented in your subconscious as to be stronger and more sure than everyone else's cynicism and doubt*.

When in control of your life in this way, you will become calm and self-assured, untouched and untainted by negative forces. You will be aware of your positive aura drawing other like-inclined souls to you. You'll feel that the whole world is with you!

Unlike some others …..

~

All too common among some in modern day society is the mind-set that control of their lives and events in it lie with 'someone else' – *'the whole world is against me'* mentality - rather than accepting that they alone are responsible for their own well-being. These people establish no control over their own destinies and constantly feel sorry for themselves. In this state they often shun the help and advice of well-intentioned associates thereby alienating those well-wishers and furthering in reality their own distorted perception of being victimised!

Being a 'victim' is psychologically an all too easy opt out. It allows the practitioner to :

- *Always feel in the right*

- *Never have to make decisions or take action*

- *Often be the centre of attention of those concerned about them*

- *Never have to risk failure or rejection*

- *Always avoid the burden of responsibility*

Given that there appears to be some compelling benefits to be gained from feeling that 'the whole world is against me', why should people in general reject that mind-set? Why are self-confident and well balanced individuals in particular, inherently and vehemently opposed to it? The answer is simple. Feeling sorry for ones-self is a downward spiral to oblivion whereas accepting responsibility for all ones thoughts and deeds is a sure fire route to personal freedom.

POWER POINT - *"When you take full control of your situation and assume full responsibility for all of your thoughts and actions, success becomes a virtual certainty."*

Put another way, self-pity is a negative and therefore wasteful exercise. Assuming responsibility is, on the other hand, positive and energizing. It :

- *Frees up all the time previously wasted on wallowing in self-pity*

- *Frees one from the hurt and negativity of self-sorrow*

- *Allows the repair of damaged relationships*
- *Reignites ambition and a desire to achieve*
- *Reduces need for external validation*
- *Empowers self-confidence*
- *Builds life stability*

The old adage that *'where losers see difficulty, winners see only opportunity'* applies very much when comparing the mentalities of the 'whole world is against me' brigade with those of people at ease with themselves and the world in general.

When faced with a demanding situation, the self-confident will assume control by asking three questions of themselves.

First -

"Who is worse off than me?"

By posing this question to themselves they put the situation in perspective and thus reduces pressure on themselves, they make it easier.

Then they asks -

"What opportunity does this present?"

This is the polar opposite to wallowing in self pity and to find the answer to this question there is a third crucial question positive people will ask. It is this -

"How can I give value to others right now?"

You see, the way that you think and act towards others is fundamental to your perception of your own self-worth. Those who indulge in *'the whole world against me'* ethos are inherently selfish and thinking only of themselves. They suffer from a crucifix mentality.

Those at ease with their own character focus, by comparison, more on helping others. This they know will raise their own self-esteem and make themselves, as well as their beneficiaries, feel good. They also understand that it will ultimately, prove profitable - both spiritually and pragmatically. They look not for obstacles but for the opportunity in all situations, no matter how dire, and find it in the way that they can assist others to overcome difficulty.

POWER POINT - *"Seek opportunity in ways to assist others to overcome adversity."*

Note however, that self-confident people are not only good to others, they are good to themselves too. So be nice to yourself. Start by asking, *"Why is the world such a wonderful place!"* ... and then write down your ten most joyful reasons for being alive. Place your list where it is prominent and visible. Recite your positive affirmations of life to yourself several times each day. You'll soon come to realise that the world is with you all the way ... you only have to open your heart to it!

Chapter 12

THINGS YOU SAY

In my positive state of mind there are certain words and expressions I use. Others I avoid. *'Value'* is a good word, I like it a lot. As in -

How can I be of value to you?

What do you most value in life?

Did I say how much I value your friendship?

Yes, the word value implies compassion and integrity, also confidence.

On the other hand, the word *'problem'* I never use. It crops up all the time. To me it's a negative expression. It implies worry. Such as -

I have a problem at work or *I've got money problems* etc.

To so many people life is just a series of never ending problems.

But to those of a positive mind and sunny disposition the idea of a *'problem'* doesn't exist! They speak instead of *'situations'*. They recognise life as simply a series of evolving situations. Each one a challenge demanding action yes, but which, when resolved, simply leads to the next situation – and so on.

Viewed thus, there are no problems – and therefore nothing to worry about! There is no stress or conflict in life as being in a situation is the normal state of being.

Think and talk only situations. Then you will be of positive value to yourself and will be highly valued by others too!

POWER POINT - "Being in a situation is the normal state of being!"

Among the expressions which I avoid to the point of having totally erased them from my mind (well until now at least), "It's not my fault," and "I'm bored!" are two which I find most loathsome.

When someone says, "It's not my fault!", it generally means that it is! Well balanced, responsible individuals never say this. They accept full responsibility for their own actions and for events in and surrounding their own lives. They know that they alone create entirely the life that is theirs.

Such people do not subscribe to the popular belief of many that our lives are somehow forced upon us or are created for us by others. They believe instead in self-determination and freedom of thought and expression. The first place that positive minded people always look when questioning events affecting them is – in the mirror!

POWER POINT - *"The first place that personally responsible people look when questioning events affecting them is ... in the mirror!"*

This ability of personally aware people to be self-critical and analytical is one of their great strengths. This is what taking responsibility is all about, not blaming someone else.

"It's not my fault", is a cop out, an abdication of responsibility and, yes, it's childish. It denies the simple truth that almost any event that may occur to us at any time, anywhere in our lives, our businesses, our relationships is brought about or triggered by our own actions.

When a person takes it upon themselves to be responsible for themselves, their situation, all of their thoughts and deeds and for their whole life then they have taken the first and most important step towards achieving control of their lives. They become better human beings and valued members of society.

Whenever I hear the words "I'm bored" uttered, it not only makes me angry but also fills me with disbelief. I just cannot comprehend how any remotely intelligent being could ever be bored. In fact I point-blank refuse to acknowledge the existence of the state of boredom.

As a kid I was the exact opposite of today's desk-shackled computer generation. I was forever on the move. Life was a blur of constant action and remains so to this day. There simply are not enough hours in a day, days in a week, weeks in a year or years in a lifetime for me to do everything that needs doing and all the things I want to achieve … but I have a damned good try!

Those who claim boredom are just not trying. If they looked they'd find plenty to do, if not for themselves then for others. Put it this way … How could anyone be bored when there are so many people out there needing help? The old, the sick, the lonely and the disadvantaged. To anyone who says they're bored, I say, "Find someone less fortunate than yourself to help and give of your time to them.

POWER POINT - *"Find those less fortunate than yourself to help and to give of your time to."*

When you do that you'll find that not only are your days filled but you yourself will be fulfilled. There will simply be no place in your life for "I'm bored!"

~

So, there are certain words and expressions you should use regularly and there are others which you should never use and must eradicate all memory of. But precisely why? Let's take a closer look.

It is the words that you use in every day speech which give you the ability to communicate your thoughts to other people. Without verbal exchanges we would be limited to conveying what is in our mind by reproducing the pictures which we see in our mind's eye.

Were you to do that, present a picture image rather than a word format of your thoughts to others, then all recipients would see exactly the same picture. What you were 'saying' would be perfectly clear and appear exactly the same to every observer. But would it? Would each individual interpret what they were seeing in the same way?

If that image were, for example, the iconic Leonardo da Vinci painting of Mona Lisa, some might indeed see the enigmatic smile, the subtle modelling of forms and the atmospheric illusionism attributed to the work by art afficionados. Others might simply see a not very pretty face and little else. Beauty indeed is in the eye of the beholder! Appreciation and understanding of what is being presented is very much in the *perception* of the beholder.

While all viewers might agree that they were looking at a painting their opinion as to what they were seeing could vary dramatically. If something as apparently straightforward and clear as a tangible work of art can be so open to many interpretations then, likewise, thoughts conveyed to others in picture form could equally be open to multiple interpretations. There would be no one unequivocal meaning received by all. To complicate matters more, the 'painter' himself might have intended many meanings too!

On the other hand, when you use speech you translate your picture images into sounds and words in order to convey your thoughts to others. Does verbal communication eliminate all possible confusion? Unfortunately not, not nearly. Yet it does vastly improve matters because with language you have at your disposal a vast arsenal of words and expressions with which to much more closely define the meanings and nuances which you intend. You can articulate an altogether more precise message! There are difficulties too -

* The sheer volume of words available

* How the words are used

* The many expressions, colloquialisms, dialects and accents

* Mannerisms accompanying the words

* How the speaker is perceived by the recipient

* The subliminal message conveyed by the words' use

–   and it is the last of these, the subliminal message inherent in our choice of words and expressions, that is most significant in revealing to others how you view yourself and therefore how they will perceive you.

Therefore, when conversing with others it is of utmost importance that you :

* *Limit yourself to simple words and phrases*

* *Use short sentences*

* *Avoid colloquialisms*

** Speak calmly and clearly*

In addition to that, study your own body movements, the signals that often accompany speech. Learn to keep your body, hand, eye movements natural and consistent with what you are saying or listening to. Keep your message consistent with what you already know about the other party and with how well they know you!

By working and improving on these points you can become a better communicator. One who is recognised for your clarity of message and from that, crucially, one whose word is trusted! Yes, the two go together. Once you become recognised as a trustworthy person then you feel good about yourself!

POWER POINT - *"Expressing yourself with simple clarity and self assurance will earn the respect and trust of others."*

Let's look more deeply at the subliminal message conveyed by the words that you use.

The Subliminal Message In Your Words

By 'subliminal' we mean something which you think, say or do but of which you are unaware (it is sub-conscious). In this case the way in which your use of certain words or expressions might create unintended, unwanted or negative perceptions of you or your intentions in your audience or which might divulge inner aspects of yourself which you do not wish to. Let's recap on that :

The subliminal message in what you say might :

* Give a bad, unintended or negative impression of yourself

* Reveal secret aspects of yourself

Now, unless you are of a peculiarly masochistic persuasion (and I'll assume for the purpose of this text that you're not), I'd suggest that you want to create the exact opposite effect when in dialogue with your peers. I will assert in fact that what you want to convey in your conversation is to :

* Give a good, positive impression of yourself and

* Protect those of your inner secrets which you wish to

The good news is that you can accomplish these aims by learning to use only positive language and in the ways mentioned earlier. Of course, what you say must be true. Just learning the correct things to say is not enough. It's a start but to be long term effective and, most importantly, believable, then you yourself must believe in what you are saying. That means acting out your 'good self' in your daily life, work and being. It means implanting in your subconscious that this is the real you and that the words which you use to portray yourself are therefore true also.

POWER POINT - *"Only when you believe what you say will others believe you."*

The words must align with your actions and become so embedded in your subconscious that they are the expressions which accurately relate to you and which are automatically released at any time of asking.

When you profoundly perceive yourself as the person represented by those words then everyone else will perceive you in that light too!

Chapter 13

THINGS YOU DO

As well as the things that you say being critical to who you are, the things that you do are if anything, of even greater importance. Actions, after all, speak louder than words! For the things that you say to be believable to others and for the subliminal message you convey in your interactions to be consistent with those words then your words themselves must be consistent with your actions.

How others perceive you is going to be even more influenced by seeing what you do rather than just hearing it. Again 'though it is important that you truly believe in what you're doing rather than just going through the motions in order to impress. That fools no-one, least of all yourself. Put your heart into your endeavours and particularly give thought as to ways in which you can positively interact with others.

Following are some simple and practical examples of ways to go about this both verbally and actually :

Are You Giving Attention?

We are all familiar with the question, "Are you paying attention?", probably first heard from a teacher in school days as our mind wandered to the week-end, football, girls, cars or unmentionable mischief in the planning. We certainly heard it in adolescence from parents and later from bosses and others too. But have you ever been asked, "Are you *giving* attention?" Probably not, it's just not a common wording of the question.

Yet it's a wording packed with deeper meaning. A phrasing of the question, your understanding of which is crucial to your success as a human being. It's a question which you need to ask of yourself. Because it has been said that giving attention to others, as in bestowing a gift, is the rarest and purest form of generosity. So you should gift your attention extravagantly! Are you giving attention?

POWER POINT - *"Giving attention to others is the rarest and purest form of generosity."*

Communication you see, is a two way process. It is not just equally important to give attention and respect to what others have to say. It is more important. After all, if you give attention to other people then they are more likely to do like wise with you!

That's not to say that what you have to say is of lesser importance than the other person's views. It's just that you will learn more by listening than you ever will by speaking. Ration your own input to conversations and instead nudge the other person to speak by use of little prompts and questions. Show genuine interest in what they have to say and take in the flood of information which will come your way. Don't interrupt their flow or finish off sentences for them. Just listen.

Yet it's a common fault when listening to others to not actually be engaged in what they are saying. You will find your mind wandering, often searching frantically for your own version of, or a story or experience similar to, the dialogue being delivered by the speaker. That is not listening. You're learning nothing from it. Be aware of this shortcoming (everyone suffers from this to some degree), rein in your imagination and really concentrate on the words of the other person. Give them your full attention. Consciously or unconsciously they will pick up on your interest and at some point will ask for your view or opinion At that point you can have your say.

Then, when you speak, be brief and crystal clear. Always be absolutely straightforward and to the point. Say exactly what you feel. Those who mind about what you say don't matter and those who matter won't mind.

POWER POINT - *"Those who mind about what you say don't matter and those who matter won't mind."*

Up until that point, when you feel tempted to interrupt just take a deep breathe and relax. In the case of finding yourself in the company of a totally self-centred bore, hogging the conversation, simply excuse yourself and leave.

Often you will find that differences of opinion arise in conversation. Remember that opinions are just that. There is no right or wrong. It's practically inevitable that you will learn something of some kind from what is said and is in the other opinion. There will be some truth there. On that basis there's no requirement on your part to either defend your own position or to criticise that of the other party.

Be generous to the other party. If they insist on being 'right' then allow them to be. By doing so you are being kind rather than right. Others will remember and relate to your kindness long after they've forgotten the 'right opinion' of another. If you must choose between being kind and being right, choose being kind and you will always be right!

Thank people for their opinion, views or information imparted - "Wow I didn't know that, thanks!" Be enthusiastic and find genuine ways to compliment them. "Boy, that took courage!" Tell them what it is that you like or admire in what they've said or in what they do. Let them have the glory!

Resist any urge to criticise ... ever. Should you find yourself or what you have to say criticised by others then, rather than defend your position, agree with them! Use self-effacing humour of the "What do I know?" variety and see how people positively respond to it. It's far more effective and more fun than confrontation. It will win you respect and friends too.

Random Acts Of Kindness

It's common for people to have in mind to perform charitable or other acts of compassion for others but to be thinking on a grand scale. Raising money or awareness through a single-handed rowing of the Atlantic, thousand mile mountain trek or something of that nature. As a result they never get around to doing it. Their good intent slips away. Truth is that in most cases their ambition was totally unrealistic and as such always a non-starter. Nothing gets done. Nobody benefits.

Those, on the other hand, who think small often end up achieving great things (that is itself a general recipe for 'success') and the small acts themselves can have an immense impact on the lives of others. Also, small intents are far more likely to be acted out simply because they are easy and quick to accomplish.

There's a multitude of small things that you can perform on a daily basis which are nothing more than random acts of kindness but which can impress hugely on the lives of recipients, uplift your own spirit and create general joy and goodwill.

In respect of general kindness, don't wait for others to engage with you (you might wait forever)! Take the initiative and perform some small service for that elderly neighbour, infirm acquaintance or overworked mother. Take out their dustbin, help them cross the road, carry their shopping. It needn't be much but do something of the kind at least once per day, that's all it takes.

Neither expect nor ask for anything in return. That misses the point altogether. So too does telling others or 'bragging' about your good work. This reeks of doing it for recognition or plaudits and completely un-does the goodness of the act in respect of your spiritual well-being. Show humility, not just with these acts of random kindness but in everything that you do. Recognise the fragility and preciousness of human life and help others to protect that and their dignity too.

Healthy Negative Thoughts

What you first think, you become. When you constantly think negative thoughts then you, your life and what you are will become negative too. It's better to learn to generate thoughts which are positive and productive.

This process however includes the necessity to be able to deal with and manage, perfectly healthy negative thoughts. Healthy negative thoughts? ... what the heck is that? Well it's all to do with emotions. Let me explain.

Everyone experiences emotions. There is nothing wrong in that. There are no good or bad emotions, just emotions. But certain emotions are often regarded as being negative. I'm thinking of fear and anger predominantly. Of course these are neither negative nor un-necessary feelings. They exist to perform the vital function of protecting you. When people speak of them in a negative way, what they are really talking about is the way in which people handle the emotions, not the emotions themselves.

The point is that a healthy you is going to experience feelings of anger and fear (and others) anyway but negativity is connected with how you handle the emotions, not the emotions themselves. You must harness the energy of the anger or fear or whatever in a positive way. You can allow the emotion to consume you like a character in a TV soap or you can lighten up, put them in perspective and get on with the not at all unimportant task of enjoying life!

POWER POINT - *"There are no negative or positive emotions, only positivity or negativity in the way that you deal with them."*

You need to remember that all thoughts, be they a strong emotional one or a simple memory, are just thoughts. They can't touch or harm you. Unless you churn them over again and again until you convince yourself that you are unhappy, ill even.

Understand that a thought may be in your mind but, unless it's relevant to what you're doing at the precise moment, it is only a memory of or reaction to a past event or a precursor to a future one. In either case the events are not real time events. They are no longer actual or they have yet to become actual.

By recognising the existence of this time distance between your thoughts and the events they represent, you can relax and put aside any anxiety you might feel. The strategy is simply to dismiss from your mind the troublesome thought and with it dispel all the 'negative' feelings surrounding it. Your cleared and clear mind thus created can then address and deal with matters from a calm, unobstructed perspective, devoid of negative influence. You can get on with enjoying life!

I Love You But ...

I remember in my youth being attracted to girls predominantly because of some particular aspect of their physical appearance or movement. Personality came into it too but at that age it was a distant secondary consideration!

Whatever the attraction, once 'going steady' with a girl, I'd inevitably find that a few weeks into the relationship I would become aware of some aspect of her persona which didn't quite fit with the picture I carried in my mind of how my perfect girl-friend should be. Whether what irritated me was in her appearance, dress, make up, habits, mannerisms, preferences or who she spoke to, I'd quickly set about trying to change her! I'd issue a lot of not so subtle, *"Why do you do ... ?"*, *"Do you know you tend to ... "* and *"Can't you be more ... "* hints.

At this point I can hear you all groaning in unison, "Big mistake!" and grimacing. Quite right of course and easy for all you sat there in your smug tartan dressing gowns of mature experience. But look around and you'll find in alarmingly close proximity to you, those of your kin or of your acquaintance who, despite their wisdom of years, are practicing the very same foolhardiness with regard to their partners as I did with girl-friends in my formative years. They are guilty as I was of focusing on the imperfections in their relationships rather than appreciating the beauty.

What's more I'd suggest that you know people who practice this negative behaviour in many areas of their lives. People who are constantly looking for what they don't like or what they find disagreeable with their friends, their work, their lives, with society, with the world! People who are griping and constantly critical.

Now - imagine that you were to quite deliberately employ exactly the opposite philosophy!

Imagine that you consciously sought out and embraced only the agreeable, pleasant and pleasing aspects of your life, the people in it, your work and all around you. Wouldn't that make you yourself feel happier and lighter and also a more appealing personality for others to be around? Wouldn't it just create an altogether more pleasant world for everyone?

POWER POINT - *"Choose to dwell only on positives and you'll create a happy world all around you."*

Behaving thus, it's true that you might be accused by those same doubters and nay-sayers referred to, of being overly optimistic and of viewing life through rose tinted spectacles. What's wrong with that? You'd also be recognised as a happy and contented person, one at ease with yourself and your world. You'd be known as a person of laughter and joy.

I myself learned quite quickly that I was missing out on a lot in the girl-friend department because of my shallow attitude. In the interim I have benefited greatly from looking for, and finding, only the good things in personal relationships with the opposite sex and more generally in all situations. You can too!

Whoever you are, whatever your situation, take time to consciously consider all that is good in your life and especially in your loved ones, your relationships and in all the people you know or meet. Write down all their attractive points, the positives and the benefits they bestow - that's a good way to cement them in your mind – and pin the list where you can see and be reminded of it daily. When you do this it will change forever the light in which you view all those around you. Especially your girl-friends/boy-friends!

Instant Gratitude

We live in an era of instant gratification. The internet and smart phones ensure that information, entertainment, communications, purchases and almost any personal or corporate whim or desire can be delivered instantly at the touch of a screen. In fact the whole tenor of modern life demands that every need and experience must be satisfied now! A generation has grown up who know and expect nothing less.

Are they grateful for what they have, the volume and speed of it, the freedoms they enjoy? Or do they take them for granted? Do they ever think to give thanks for the fact that everything comes so easily to them, that they don't have to endure the pain of manual labour or the hardship of going without basic necessities of life? Do they match their insatiable lust for instant gratification with expressions of *instant gratitude?*

I suspect not and that's a shame. Because being thankful, showing your appreciation, expressing gratitude is a basic act of human decency. It's a celebration of life and the people in it, most powerful when given spontaneously.

React instantly and positively when someone gifts you their time, their love, their devotion, something material or assistance of any kind. Thank life on a daily basis for the many good things which it bestows.

Here are some tips :

* Ingrain it in your sub-conscious that you will always say a pleasant "Thank you" for even the most minor of kindnesses. Make it second nature.

* Actively seek out those to whom you are due a "thank you" for some recent or past kindness rather than just waiting for a suitable moment to arise. That moment may never come! With time you might forget altogether the gratitude owed. The other party won't. They'll remember that you never thanked them, see

you as ungrateful and will harbour resentment against you. An unfortunate downward spiral in your relationship might occur. So seek them out and say "Thank you" - do it now!

* Go with an expression of gratitude to other people to whom you're not due a particular "Thank you" but who positively influence you or your life on an ongoing, or even occasional, basis. Think each day of at least one person who qualifies in this way and go tell them, "Thank you!" They'll be pleasantly surprised, mighty pleased and your relationship with them will be positively boosted. Everyone will feel good!

* While you're at it, tell people what it is about them that you like, appreciate or admire. People just love to receive compliments! Think about it. How often in your life have you felt neglected or that some act, achievement or ability went unacknowledged? Well you can bet that others have experienced similar disappointmet at times too. Can you imagine how good, how appreciated they will feel when you turn up out of the blue with a, *"That was a great thing you did, really courageous ... "* or similar. It can quite literally light up their lives. The spin off is that it will brighten your day too!

* Remember that gratitude is a positive emotion. When you activate it by consciously thinking of people to whom you owe or could show gratitude, you ignite in yourself the feel good factor of doing something worthwhile. The recipients of your goodwill are likewise turned on by your consideration. They absorb and feed off the positive zing you've created. Everyone is joyful. It's win win!

* Include people for whom you feel love or who love you. Don't wait for a romantic moment or some future time. Go to them daily and express your gratitude for them and for their love. Think of friends to whom this applies, relatives and those who you may

not have seen or had contact with for a long time. Make it a daily habit to make one such contact. You"ll be amazed once you put your mind to it at just how many people there are who care about you but haven't made the effort or had the courage to tell you. Don't wait for them, take the initiative. Find them and tell them of your love. Thank them for being there. You can do it by telephone, in person is better. Or you can write ...

* Write, and I mean hand write, a note of thanks for any kindness awarded to you. Hand deliver your message to the recipient rather than post it. I don't feel that I need to demonstrate just how powerful such an act of gratitude carried out in this way can be ... but ... following is the text of just such a message which I received some years ago. The writer scribbled it on the back of an envelope which is today framed and displayed in my study. It is before me as I write. I rank it among my most valuable possessions and the one of which I am most proud. It reads :

"Dear Tom,

It might come as a surprise but I am truly lost for words to express my gratitude to you for all you have done for me over the last few weeks. Your support, advice and company were immeasurable during these tough times.

Your offer of friendship so generously given to someone you didn't know will never be forgotten.

Remembering one of our many conversations I feel compelled to share the words following :

A song, a line of poetry, a sermon or a flower

Will seem to hold special meaning in the darkest hour.

An unexpected gift, a friendly deed from one unknown

A smile, a sympathetic word, a little kindness shown.

It's strange how just a simple thing can help us on our way

And strengthen us and hearten us throughout the weary day.

And so through human agency God's purpose is unrolled

He works in deep mysterious ways his secrets to unfold.

In every good and lovely thing some hidden meaning lies

The stranger at your door may be an angel in disguise.

Many thanks, Ann."

I have never seen myself as an angel (my late parents and former school teachers would fall about in uncontrollable laughter at the thought)! Regardless, I appreciated the opportunity presented me by circumstance to be of assistance to 'Ann' (you know who you are) the writer of the note. More so, I'm eternally grateful for and personally enhanced by her recognition. It humbles me.

To this day, I can barely describe how I felt when I received and first read that letter. It did bring me to tears. I felt so loved and appreciated. It made me want to give even more of myself and more of my time to more people. It was one of the moments that I fully realised that only by practicing compassion and forgiveness in my life would I truly find personal joy and fulfillment.

Gratitude you see, genuine gratitude, comes from the heart of the sender. It invokes in its recipients the most wonderful reactions and responses such as mine which I've related here. It transmits with potent force an energy of the most positive and humane kind. It creates warmth and deep contentment in everyone, sender or recipient, who is exposed to it.

So I urge you, be kind to others. Show them that you care. Tell them of your love and of your appreciation for all that they are and all that they do. Thank them. Do it daily. Do it now! *Practice instant gratitude.*

Chapter 14

SHOW A LITTLE KINDNESS

I froze outside the door of my ground floor apartment. My key would not turn in the lock, a sure sign of an intruder within. I went quickly to the storage cupboard on the stairwell and retrieved a heavy monkey-wrench to use as a weapon if need be and shoulder charged through the door ... just in time to see my thief exiting head first through the open kitchen window. I dived after him but caught only a shoe in my hand. He hobbled off minus the footwear, down the garden and over the wall to freedom.

A quick look around revealed no obvious losses. The television, hi-fi and alcohol, customary targets of the opportunist burglar, were all in place. I had clearly arrived home just after he had made his entry. I surveyed the damage I had inflicted on my own front door and temporarily replaced such wood splinters as I could. Then I went upstairs to inquire of neighbours if any had seen or heard anything, or if indeed they themselves had been victims.

As I stopped outside the door of my immediate upstairs neighbour her son, a young lad frequently in scrapes and who I knew casually, entered the building. On seeing me, the first thing he did was ask for his shoe back!

At that exact moment I realised for the first time that it was he who had broken into my apartment. He realised in the same instant that I had not seen his face nor otherwise recognised him as he fled across the garden! Simultaneous with that, his mother opened the door of her apartment and asked what the heck was going on!

As the shoe fiasco easily established that he was the guilty party, he quickly confessed and offered profuse apologies (he was actually a rather likeable if somewhat wayward lad). It transpired that he had only earlier that same morning been released from the local prison having served two weeks for his most recent misdemeanour, a small matter of 'borrowing' someone's wallet from the pocket of their coat at the local pub.

His mother was enraged. She smacked him hard round the side of his head with the grill pan that happened to be in her hand when she answered the door. She dragged him inside by his ear, begging me as she did so not to call the police and assuring me that she would deal with the matter and that he would suffer. Judging by the bedlam and screaming that roared from the apartment after the door closed, I've little doubt that suffer he did. I left his shoe outside their door … and I didn't call the police!

Was I wise not to report him? Who knows. I know that I did grant him a kindness, one from which I hope he benefited in later life. I certainly did. Because rightly or wrongly I did a fellow human a good turn and, one way or another, life has a habit of returning to you what you dish out. It maybe wasn't the right decision to be so lenient but it was the kind one. If faced with being right or being kind, I believe that choosing kind means that you're always right!

POWER POINT - *"When faced with being right or being kind, choosing kind means that you'll always be right!"*

I myself had been a wild lad. In youth I'd been in more than my fair share of scrapes. On more than one occasion I could have found myself in serious trouble. Fortunately there were those who believed in me, gave me the benefit of the considerable doubt which my escapades created and either let me, or got me, off the hook. It's a funny thing but, while I don't particularly remember all the dreadful acts I perpetrated nor all the people who suffered as a consequence, I do remember vividly each and every one of the people who were generous to me and kind.

So remember in your own life to be kind to people in all sorts of ways. This isn't to say that you shouldn't report crimes committed by people you know. Such a policy would be foolhardy and potentially dangerous to others. But you can be compassionate and exercise discretion when deciding if it's possible to show a little kindness to someone or give them a break.

Your decision could get an unfortunate or misdirected being back on track and totally change the course of their lives. That person will remember and relate to your kindness long after they've forgotten other people and events. With the memory of your compassion to console them, they need never feel lonely.

~

Do you ever feel lonely? Do you know what is loneliness? Do you know the difference between being physically alone, mentally alone and spiritually alone? It's a real teaser of a question. It's one that many people struggle with because they really cannot differentiate between the three. To them physically alone is equal to mentally alone is equal to loneliness and the inertia of energy which comes with it; and spiritual loneliness they rarely even consider. But it is this last, spiritual loneliness, which is the key to the whole 'Do you ever feel lonely?' question. Once you understand spiritual loneliness and address the issue, then it is really quite simple to confront loneliness in the wider sense.

The standard fix for what people perceive to be physical and/or mental loneliness is to socialise, go to pubs or restaurants or to any place where there is a lot of people, noise and activity; the supposition being that this will stimulate, invigourate and fill the void in their lives. Short term and up to a point this can work but the major drawback with this approach is that it doesn't resolve the underlying difficulty and therefore, in the longer term, inevitably makes matters worse. Such superficial physical company devoid of any real and meaningful, close or emotional connection simply deepens the scar in your well-being and increases your distress. It creates neither security nor understanding and takes its toll on your spiritual character.

It is there within your spiritual being that you need to look for the solutions. It is your inner spirit which must be nourished in order to eliminate feelings of isolation or loneliness which you experience in your mental and/or physical existence. Initiate the process by practicing the joyous and generous behaviours I speak of throughout my text. First it's necessary to understand that being alone isn't necessarily a bad thing. You need to recognise the good which solitude can do to create ease within yourself.

POWER POINT - *"Being alone isn't necessarily a bad thing. You need to recognise the good which solitude can do to create ease within yourself."*

You may not need as much social contact as you think you do. And certainly not of the superficial, meaningless kind. Most of the time you can do just fine when alone. The rest of the time seek out opportunities and relationships which will satisfy your more profound emotional and intellectual needs.

When thus satisfied you are self aware and relaxed, with a balanced psyche at ease with both solitude and society. You'll tend to shun the superficial and embrace life's simple pleasures. You'll be a better person for it. You will draw to you genuine people, meaningful relationships and rewarding situations.

This is because you are like a magnet. Your underlying feelings and beliefs are what attract people to, or repel people from, you. When you believe yourself to be unattractive or undeserving then you will draw into your life people who reflect those feelings and treat you badly. When you know that you are loving and kind then you will draw to you lovely people who shower you with kindness. How you perceive yourself is how others perceive you!

Everyone subconsciously transmits energy. Some emit positive energy with the power to attract, others send out negative energy pulses which cause positively inclined people to move away. Where the energy is neither one nor the other, or a mix of the two, then it is neutral.

The first-mentioned positive energy people are (broadly speaking) those effervescent, bubbly types, full of energy, fun and interesting to be with. If at a party they are the one with a crowd around them orchestrating the conversation and entertaining. In daily life they'll be busy too. Always working on projects and ideas, stimulating thought and action in those around them and generally finding things to do, situations to improve and people to help. You'll find such a person to be warm, sociable and likeable. 'Infectious' is the term often applied to them; that is they infect you with their positive spirit and stimulate you to be likewise.

Negative energy can infect you too. But it's more akin to a contagious disease! It soaks out from and around people of the negative energy category like a dark cloud. Hence the reason that such people should be 'avoided like the plague'. Contact with them is likened to contracting a disease and is characterised by the spreading of negative qualities such as depression, greed, selfishness and inner anger. That's precisely why they repel content, happy people but draw in those of a similarly critical, hostile or low self-esteem personality.

Neutral energy people tend to be a bit of both but generally neither. They won't lack confidence entirely but neither will they be exuberant in their demeanour. They'll have a degree of ego but won't display it. They'll be indifferent and lack firm opinions. They'll merge into the background rather than appear in the limelight. They'll be grey.

Whichever of those three – positive, negative, neutral – applies to you then you can be sure that you will attract into your life people and situations of the same ilk. The law of attraction states that like attracts like. If some aspect of your world is not as you wish it to be then you must examine your inner being and change the way that you feel about yourself. Once you do that you will attract an accordingly different set of people, circumstances and experiences to you and you will do it sub-consciously on auto pilot.

Look around you. Look at the situations pertaining to your life and the characters in it. They are there for a reason. The underlying cause of their being there is that you have invited them in. If you now feel that they are unwelcome and do not represent the way that you want your life to be then you must evict them. To do that you must re-set your inner magnet!

You must change your inner thoughts and underlying beliefs to attract into your life the situations and people who you wish to have there.

POWER POINT - *"Attract into your life only joyous situations and kind people who you wish to have there."*

Once you have elements of love, joy, kindness and generosity installed in your inner being and radiating with high frequency from you and everything that you do, then you will attract into your life people and situations on the same energy level.

The law of attraction is a remarkably simple law of nature, of human existence. You can send out negative energy and have misery engulf you or you can choose to radiate brilliance and bask in its golden glow!

Now you know that you yourself, whether consciously aware of it or not, create everything that is in your life. You choose one way or another the people around you, your trade or profession, your hobbies and pursuits and every other thing about your being. This includes your beliefs, feelings and emotions.

You can elect to enjoy a happy life brimming with love, joy and friendship or opt for a miserable existence of self-loathing, being judgemental and critical of others and mean towards them. It's up to you.

POWER POINT - *"It's your choice alone as to whether you enjoy a happy life or a miserable one."*

Whatever your choice, first you must have a vision. This is often refered to as a dream or as imagination. Either way, you must have a picture in your mind of who you want to be, what you want to be and how you want to be.

If your vision of yourself is of a negative, discontented being then that is what you will be. It's clearly better by far that you create a bright, positive image of your present and future self because that, by the same token, is what you will become.

Unfortunately, many with this good, healthy dream for themselves still fail to achieve the happy state they envisage. There are two reasons for this and they often go together. The first is :

*** They don't write down their plan for themselves and they don't state it out loud to themselves several times every day**

The second is :

*** Even if they have established their plan, they have not done so with clarity**

… and clarity means two things :

*** Being absolutely crystal clear about your intentions**

and

*** Stating it in fine detail**.

Even a small detail left out of your plan, or a statement of intent which is not absolutely specific may mean that it is not possible to achieve that which you intend. Worse still, its omission may lead to a totally different interpretation of your dream being placed in, and acted on, by your subconscious.

In my book, *'Mastering the Art of Making Money'*, I refer to a material manifestation of this principle when talking of preparing a business plan. I refer to the plan as requiring the fine detail of what is intended to be clearly defined. In what I call the *'I Want'* section of the document I urge readers to state what it is, in material or spiritual terms, that they want to get from the project. In the case in question I stress that stating your want as a Mercedes limousine is not sufficient. Rather you must state the exact model, year, condition, colour, trim etc. In other words every fine detail of the car you wish to own.

Another good illustration of the concept is the fishing analogy. Asking just for a fish could catch you anything from a sardine to a shark. So be careful what you ask for! If it's a tasty piece of salmon you're after then say just that. Describe the salmon, the bait to use, where to catch it and when. Then, all being well, it will be salmon that you end up with on your plate.

So with life. Be specific. You must ask of it exactly and in detail, precisely what you want. More so than mere material things or monetary wealth, this is of greatest significance with regard to your spiritual ambitions and the human being that you want to be.

When, for example, you want to better yourself by giving more of yourself to others (and that is a fine intention) then you will want to write that down. First it's important to know that you must *always write in the present tense*. By so doing you are telling yourself that you already are what you say you are and your sub-conscious will take that in and incorporate it as fact. You will write, "I *am* good to others," rather than "I will be … "

While that statement alone is excellent to use as a daily mantra repeated out loud, it does not detail how, where, when and to whom you are being good! Your written vision statement must be stated with greater clarity. It must include all the detail of the who, where, when and how you are good to others – the more detail the better. Then your sub-conscious will zero in on exactly these commands as to what is required.

Now place your written plan in a prominent place where you will see it continuously. Take time to read it through slowly and calmly each day. Absorb ever more deeply the message and instructions you have prepared for yourself. Each day repeat aloud to yourself, morning and night, the brief headline mantras applying to your wider vision.

In addition, express with clarity to the world all that you say and do. This includes being truthful and honest and acting with integrity so that others know without doubt or confusion exactly who you are and what you stand for.

Behaving in this way may at times not please certain people but those likely to mind don't matter and those who matter won't mind.

Never think in terms of pleasing everyone. It's not possible. Trying to do so is the route to certain failure. Your mission is not to please people with respect to whether they like you or not, your mission is to be self-confident and true to yourself and through that earn the respect of others.

POWER POINT - *"The route to certain failure is to try to please everyone. Aim only to earn their respect."*

Those who doubt your integrity need not be in your life at all. They will by definition be negative influences intent on draining your energy and wishing to draw you into their destructive ways.

On the other hand, by planning and acting with clarity, you will attract to you well-intentioned and well motivated enrichers and positive minded enablers who will fuel your self esteem and help drive you to the realisation of your vision.

Chapter 15

FEAR OF SECRETS

Two of the most basic human emotions are fear and love. They reside within you all the time. While these feelings can and do at times activate naturally or unconsciously beyond your control, you can make a conscious decision to live your life according to one or the other. You can choose to live your life in fear or you can choose to live your life in love. Which is it to be?

Fear in the broad sense is like a road block, a paralysis. It is typified by inflexibility of thought and action. It manifests as resistance to expressing your whole self, physically, mentally and spiritually. It is a straight-jacket holding you back from realising your full, glorious potential.

When your positive spirit and emotions are thus suppressed, you become tense and inflexible, exposed to ever more negative and undesirable emotional and behavioural traits. Resentment, hurt, anger, unkind thoughts and jealousy can all flow unabated from the personality of someone who is locked in such a state of permanent anxiety and worry. A dark aura envelopes them and drives people away from them.

A loving personality transmits, on the other hand, an altogether quite different aura. One of high energy and magnificence! Whereas fear permits the inflow of all that is negative in life, an aura of love does just the opposite. It is like a shield which keeps you safe from all harm and which actively repels destructive emotions and their insidious malignancy. More than that, an aura of love behaves like a magnet, drawing caring and positive people to you and creating around you an ever bigger family of the like-inclined.

Such people tend to behave spontaneously. Rather than fretting over matters, be they of consequence or be they trivialities, they listen to their own intuition and act accordingly. They are happy, calm, patient and radiate vitality.

These are qualities with which every single living human is endowed. It is there in your inner spirit. This deepest part of your being knows exactly what is right and what is wrong, what is good and what is bad. Regardless of parenting, education, indoctrination, culture or so-called grooming, this is an absolute constant.

POWER POINT - *"Everyone knows deep inside themselves what is right and what is wrong – that includes you!"*

Everyone knows deep down for example that it is wrong to kill another person. Most people listen to their inner voices and choose not to. So those who do kill another human do it by choice. Let's face it, it's an easy choice to make to be cowardly, aggressive or murderous. There are many of the last-inclined abroad in the world today, behaving despicably and trumpeting the same tired old line 'that a higher power instructed them' to perpetrate their ghastly crimes. Whatever excuse they may use to justify their hideous acts though, they know full well that they are kidding themselves, that their inner being cannot be fooled. They know that what they do is just plain wrong.

In the same way, every living person knows intuitively that being happy is preferable to being sad or in despair. The sure route to real happiness of the deepest most meaningful kind is to help and be kind to others. So bathe those around you in your clarity of thought and action and in the fragrance of your love and compassion. Encourage them to do likewise and to :

* Act with integrity

* Be forgiving and kind

* Live life, laugh and love!

In doing so you, and they, will have chosen to live your lives in love rather than in fear. You will have discovered that real happiness and contentment flows from that love. There's no secret to it!

~

A secret is defined as *'facts or feelings intentionally concealed'* or *'that which is unknown'* or *'that which is yet to be discovered'*. The latter definition often applies to people with regard to their own personalities and emotions.

It is clearly of benefit to learn about your own inner 'secrets', understand them and be able to discern between those healthy and of benefit to you and others which may be damaging to you, your relationships or your life in general.

It's necessary first to be at ease with your secrets. You should understand that the ability to keep things secret, as in enjoying privacy in certain areas of your life and being (your inner self), is an essential power that all human beings possess. It is a defensive and protective mechanism. It allows you to keep possession of experiences and feelings which you don't wish to share with others – and which would be of no benefit to either them or yourself were you to share them.

This process of secretly evaluating your life-experiences is the way you learn about yourself. It ultimately helps you to form your self-identity. Were you to have no capacity for such secrecy you would become totally vulnerable to the ways others see you. This because disclosing certain secrets leaves you open to the negative judgement of others and does nothing to enhance your worth in their eyes, nor significantly, your worth in your own eyes.

Should you recklessly divulge such personal and intimate information (as is the fashion these days with many on social media) then you compromise and devalue your own identity. The identities of those with whom you share it are, by association, devalued too.

Only by keeping certain secrets can you enjoy unqualified privacy in digesting and integrating your experiences. You can then use your experiences and self knowledge as positive future influences.

The word 'privacy' relates to natural secrecy. In this respect it is not something that needs to be disclosed. This 'privacy' definition, interestingly, goes against a lot of contemporary mood which views secrecy as being in conflict with openness and outright honesty. Yet secrecy need not be negative. It has crucial significance in your right to privacy and freedom and to how effectively and openly you conduct your life and relationships, both public and private.

The content of a secret can be anything. You may choose to hide almost any fact, feeling or behaviour. Your intention to conceal something may in certain instances even be a secret to yourself! i.e. your intention is subconscious. These latter events are ones that you need to uncover and examine in order to establish if they are 'healthy' secrets of value to you personally as matters of your own personal privacy or if they are 'toxic' secrets which are neither protecting your privacy nor being of positive benefit to yourself or to wider society.

There is nothing negative about your inner secrets where they protect your dignity, freedom, inner life and creativity. You have a right to privacy. It is a part of your natural endowment. The more that your natural need for privacy is respected and honoured by both yourself and by society in general, then the less deliberately secretive you need be.

POWER POINT - *"Honour your own right to privacy and respect the right to privacy of others."*

Come to terms with your inner secrets, get to know them. Weed out those not performing a useful function of natural privacy and nurture those which do. Knowing yourself in this way is the gateway to improving yourself and how others view you.

One final point of extreme importance. The more you study yourself and your functioning, the more apparent it should become that psychology plays a major part in pretty much everything that we say and do. If you don't come to that conclusion then you're not understanding our being at all. It will pay you to study the subject of psychology; everyone from Freud and Jung through to modern practitioners such as John Bradshaw and Oliver Sacks, I heartily recommend the writings of all of these. Read them, you'll be the better for it.

You will learn that, in order to understand others you must first understand yourself. Once you've got a handle on what makes you tick then you are far better placed to work out other people's behaviour. From there you'll be able to make real progress in learning to become the better person that you long to be.

The Road To Joyful Living!

PART 6

Cooperation

in which you share the joy of service

Joseph T.Riach

Chapter 16

LIFE AS A SERVANT

Were I to suggest that you live life as a servant, what image regarding my suggestion would immediately spring into your mind? Would you picture yourself under-valued and under-privileged, slaving laboriously in hardship and poverty for a cruel task master? Or perhaps you'd picture yourself employed as a butler or footman by a wealthy lord? Maybe you'd see yourself as an old time farm servant, struggling with the back-breaking manual grind of working on the land? or as an unwilling lackey tied to an unappreciative employer in some other equally servile, pittance pay, menial job? In all cases a bleak picture. Yet it need not be so.

What if I told you that in my case, the suggestion of living life as a servant conjures up a quite different image? .. a thoroughly bright and positive one. One where I envisage a happy, fulfilling life of joy and contentment and one of being a highly valued and respected member of society. How, I hear you say, can this be?

The Service Manager

When in business I learned that great managers see their function as being primarily to serve their employees rather than it being the other way around. Such bosses realise that the daily grunt and grind of their business is conducted further down the chain and at 'shop floor level' by real people. That is people with lives and aspirations of their own, health issues, financial concerns and families to care for. People with all the same considerations to contend with daily as the manager himself. They are human beings just as he is.

The good manager who understands this simple reality empathises. He knows that just like himself, employees harbour fears and anxieties, doubts and misgivings; so he sees his role as that of encouraging, helping and bringing out the best in them. Of enabling them to be relaxed, at ease and happy at their work and confident that their careers, their futures and their well-being are in good hands.

This entails creating an environment where people at all levels in the employment chain feel appreciated and cared for. Where they feel themselves part of a team all pulling in the same direction towards the same goals; and with opportunities to develop their individual strengths and preferences for both their own and everyone else's benefit. It's called helping them to do what they do best!

When a boss or manager assists his workforce in this way then they are stimulated to give of their best in return. They feel important, they feel loved. Everyone in the business, from the very bottom in the work chain to the top, benefits from it.

Rather than being a purely altruistic practice, it makes good commercial sense for the boss to see himself as, and to act as, servant to his workers.

Full Service

When I started out in business I was a self-employed sole trader. I worked sixteen hours a day, seven days a week. As the only employee it fell to me to do everything, from the cleaning of the toilet to conducting the executive meetings. I *was* the business in the fullest meaning of the term!

Plus, at any one time I had up to three or four part-time jobs in addition to running my enterprise.

Typically I would start at five in the morning to help in a bakery and deliver the morning rolls to local shops. Then I'd run home to be ready for work at my own business from nine until six. After that it was off to do a stint in the local pub (working that is)! until eleven at night. Then I took to the streets driving a taxi, often up to two or three in the morning.

In my business I had no option but to take on all the garbage work; the high hassle, low profit and often no pay-off work that no-one else would do, which experienced successful professionals didn't need to touch. After seven such years I had an ex-wife and a bank account in a permanent state of cardiac arrest. I also had loads of experience and my determination was undiminished.

I had also spent those years predominantly serving others! Everyone from the baker to the taxi operator and the pub landlord and all their clients. And my clients too of course. I was a servant – but a willing one.

Then within my business a change happened, gradually but it happened. Better quality work which had hitherto been denied to me started to come my way. This meant that I could start to bypass the garbage stuff. Because of this my self-esteem improved and my professional image was enhanced. This in turn led to even higher quality, bigger profit work coming to me and so on. I was still working very hard and long hours but I could discard the part-time jobs and concentrate wholly on my business.

My finances improved to a much healthier state and I could afford nice things such as a Mercedes coupé, foreign travel, a high-backed leather revolving chair … and to employ staff!

With the arrival of employees I could delegate work and concentrate my own efforts on those aspects of the business which I most enjoyed, was most skilled at and which were most meaningful in terms of earning income and growing the business. I concentrated on marketing and selling and passed the other work on to my growing army of employees. Eventually I had seventy-five staff under my control, employed in three main businesses, one of which was a chain of pre-school nurseries for kids up to age five (more about that in a moment).

I soon realised that it paid me to hire only the best. I was prepared to pay top whack in order to get and to keep top quality staff. More so than that, I came to understand that a great manager should see his function as being primarily to serve his employees rather than it being the other way around.

I took on board the responsibility of creating an environment where all my staff felt inclusive in the project and felt appreciated and cared for. Such was my success in this endeavour that in due course my business ran itself ... or rather my top quality staff ran it. I was now enjoying the rewards of the business but without being fully involved in every detail of it.

Sure, I was there, I had done the ground-work, had set up the systems and it was my business generating the income but often I hadn't even been in my high-backed leather chair! What I had been doing however was encouraging, helping and bringing out the best in my staff and enabling them to be relaxed, at ease and happy at their work; confident that their careers, their futures and their well-being were in good hands.

I had travelled full circle. I had become their servant.

This point was dramatically and amusingly brought home to me by one hilarious event. It concerned the pre-school nurseries. These businesses generated a sizeable quantity of daily garbage; mainly kitchen and food waste and ... soiled nappies. Of the last there were a lot! It was not the kind of refuse that could healthily lie around to wait for the weekly rubbish collection. Not even in the specially designated storage sheds at the far end of each nursery playground.

Having been ousted by my own staff from most daily practical functions in the businesses, I had discarded my striped suits, donned threadbare jeans and taken to attending to small stuff and odd jobs ... such as collecting and disposing of the waste. The waste of course included the nappies!

On this particular day my Mercedes was stuffed full of foul smelling waste sacks ... trunk, seats, roof, everywhere ... as I made my way to the council tip. Speeding in order to rid myself of the obnoxious cargo as quickly as possible, I passed through a police radar trap and was 'pulled'.

Approaching my car with it's window wound down the officer soon picked up on the sickly stench wafting from within and could see the horrible cargo of leaking sacks stacked everywhere. He wisely moved back and asked me to get out of the car. He was confronted by a scruffy, ragamuffin reeking of shit! I'd left my wallet with driving licence and documents in the office.

When I explained who I was and what I was about, he looked at me as the crazed maniac I quite clearly was and grimaced incredulously, "And you're doing this in a top range Merc?"

My stay at police H.Q. which followed was mercifully short. With an urgency born from the repulsive stink with which I was infecting the whole station and everyone in it, they established my identity, that I did indeed own the car and that I wasn't a long term detainee of a secure mental institution let loose for the day - then kicked me out. I was issued a warning as to transporting toxic waste in an undesignated vehicle and fined two hundred pounds.

Next day I bought a second hand Land Rover.

Are You Being Served?

I have not now for many years served in the manner described above, nor do I harbour any inclination to do so! But I remain impressed by the fact that all of us, whether aware of it or not, are servants at different points in our lives and in many ways. We alternate between being a servant and being served in both the long and the short term.

In family life, babies are first cared for and served by their parents. As the children grow they will learn servitude themselves by being required to perform chores in the household. Their school teachers will serve them and they in turn their teachers. Then once at college level they may have a part-time job in a café or diner where they will learn more of direct service and be servants to the management and to the clientele.

Then again, they will in turn be the customers in hotels, restaurants, shops and transportation where others will be performing the role of servant for them. Those servants themselves will in like fashion be customers of such establishments and will at those times be the ones served. And so on.

The reality is that everyone is constantly interchanging between being server or servant and being served. No individual need negatively see themselves as being in a state of servitude. Because whoever you are, whatever your status in society, you are continually a servant in some shape or form.

To those who do view their lives as being nought but an existence of permanent servitude then it might indeed be the case that they have become a lackey tied to an unappreciative employer in some servile, pittance pay, menial job. Some may have found themselves in a succession of such situations.

If this is the case it could be that the individual is acting out their own negative perception of themselves. That is, they have low self esteem, expect and therefore invite misery into their lives and subconsciously create the people, events and circumstances which will perpetuate their desperate situation. Or they may simply have taken a wrong turn in life. In either case they need to recognise that the responsibility is theirs to change their situation and take the appropriate action to achieve that.

Whether in a dire circumstance or not, the place to learn the deeper meaning of being a servant and to start to appreciate the real beauty of what life as a servant is all about, is within yourself.

Self Service

Most of you will agree that it is important to maintain your physical fitness. Even those of you who don't work out regularly know that it makes more sense to be fit than not to be. When your body is well exercised, nourished and in good health then you possess the energy and vitality to do all the things which life requires of you. This means that you will be in a position to help others should you choose to. If you're not fit yourself then you can't help or serve others. Simple.

Similarly, you need to be mentally strong. It's important to keep your mind alert too. As with your body, exercise and nourishment are the keys. Your diet should include foods known to be good for your circulation and for your brain. You should keep your mind nimble by consciously practicing mental exercise such as reading, doing crosswords and arithmetical puzzles and having many interests and activities.

You are the guardian of both your mind and body. Only you can protect and nurture them. You are the servant to yourself. With these two elements of your being attended to you are fit and able to attend to the third critical element - the need to take care of your inner self.

The way to nourish your inner being is by learning and practicing the true meaning of life as a servant.

Life As A Servant

I have written elsewhere that my uncompromising and dispassionate approach to life and business brought me some success but that I only experienced true joy and fulfillment once I understood and practiced compassion and forgiveness. You have read earlier in this chapter how the most effective managers in business are those who realise that their function is to serve their employees by making them feel inclusive and helping them to be the best that they can be. I have told you of how I implemented this approach in my own business and of how it helped me create a meaningful enterprise and a happy team of top quality people. I've even revealed how I, as boss, literally took on the role of servant to my staff, acted as garbage collector and got arrested for my efforts!

Now imagine that you were to put into practice these self same principles and actions on a daily basis in your personal life. Okay you can leave out the dirty nappy scenario! That apart, envisage that you set out with your primary aim in life not to be 'successful' or to make pots of money but just to help people. To help people in small ways and any ways and to help them to be the best that they can be. Can you see that, just like the business scenarios and examples of my own experience which I've presented, this is a certain route to happiness, joy and contentment? That such an approach will lift you to heights of serenity previously unimaginable? That by being a servant in such a way you will nurture and delight both your inner being and the spirits of all those who you serve?

POWER POINT - *"Nurture and delight your inner being by serving others needs and helping them to be the best that they can be."*

Make your priority in life to make time for other people, friends and strangers, embrace them all. Just like the enlightened business manager, listen to them, take on board their fears, concerns and anxieties and their ideas and ambitions too. Help them find solutions, encourage them, empathise. You must completely engage with them.

The first thing that will become apparent to you is that those with whom you engage in this way, more than anything, just want to be heard. They need to feel that they matter and that someone else cares and is really listening. All they really need is validation.

Validation is being there, a comforting arm around the shoulder, an acknowledgement that they have been heard and that their emotion has been understood. It is not critical, judgemental nor advisory. You would never say *"I know how you feel"*, you don't! Nor any *"If I were you ... "* nonsense. You're not! *"I can see that you're upset, how can I help?"* is the approach. That is empathising.

What people need is recognition. I remember as a young man being told that people value being happy at their work more highly than being well paid. "What rubbish!" I thought at the time. Not now! I've learned that happiness is by far the most important thing in life and that what creates it is neither monetary nor material wealth. The most important contributory factor is the love and appreciation of others, recognition if you like. The best way to achieve that for yourself is to give freely and unconditionally of your own love and joy to others.

By recognising people I mean letting them know that you are there for them, letting them know that you care. Ask people "How are you?" and mean it. Send hand written notes, not emails nor pre-printed cards. Give compliments and express genuine gratitude when appropriate. Have people enjoy being with you.

And accept the premise that you cannot be a whole person nor live a perfect day without doing something for someone who will never be able to repay you.

Kindness in words creates confidence and kindness in giving creates love. As a servant perform little acts of kindness for people on a regular basis. Simple things like :

* Hold the door open for someone

* Compliment a friend

* Bring a welcome gift to a new neighbour or work colleague

* Say a thank you to a soldier, fireman or medic

* Help other drivers emerge or park

* Carry someone's groceries

* Leave change at a vending machine

* Smile to people

* Send flowers to a deserving stranger

* Give up your train or bus seat

* Buy someone a coffee

Remember that everyone you meet is fighting a hard battle. Be charitable and kind to everyone - especially to those in need. Never question how someone down on their luck got into their plight. The fact that they are destitute or hungry is enough. Your reward is the knowledge that you helped someone who, for whatever reason, found it necessary to ask for (perhaps) and accept your assistance. Can you imagine how desperate you yourself would have to be in order to seek help from a stranger? Think about that.

Think about the fact that living life as a servant in such ways does not diminish or impoverish you. It does not enslave you. On the contrary it frees and empowers you. It is spiritually uplifting. The prospect should create in your mind a bright and positive picture of a happy, fulfilling life of joy and contentment. One of being a highly valued and respected member of society.

That is life as a servant!

Joseph T.Riach

Chapter 17

CARDINAL VIRTUES

George Washington Carver was born into slavery in Missouri in the early eighteen sixties. Yet he later graduated with a master's degree in botany at Iowa State Agricultural College and became the first black faculty member there. Then, for forty-seven years, Carver was head of the agriculture department at the Tuskegee Institute developing it into a strong research centre. He devised crop rotation techniques which brought him recognition and numerous honours. In an era of high racial polarization his fame reached beyond the black community. Carver was widely recognised and praised in all sectors for his talent and many achievements. Theodore Roosevelt publicly admired his work.

Even more so Roosevelt, and the community at large, admired Carver for being the fine man that he was.

His character was governed by his life as a devout Christian. Carver viewed his faith as a means of overcoming racial barriers. He was as concerned with his students' character development as he was with their intellectual studies. He encouraged them to adhere in their lives to the same moral code in which he believed and which he followed resolutely.

He called it his Eight Cardinal Virtues and they state :

* Be clean both inside and out

* Neither look up to the rich nor down on the poor

* Lose, if need be, without squealing

* Win without bragging

* Always be considerate of women, children and older people

* Be too brave to lie

* Be too generous to cheat

* Take your share of the world and let others take theirs

Now whether you choose to be religious or not ... and I have never believed that any religion has a monopoly on morality ... there is little doubt that those eight virtues form a not at all bad set of rules to live your life by. They strike me as being both moralistic and practical. It's the sort of list that only a man both intellectual and worldly wise would come up with. I like that. Carver seems like my kind of guy!

Let's look more closely at his teaching.

Be clean both inside and out

In this day and age of multiple bath rooms, power showers, spas and a multi-million dollar toiletries industry, not to mention the whole health and well-being phenomenon which includes bodily cleanliness too, it is probably not necessary to stress the need for good personal hygiene as might have been the case in Carver's day.

But, while standards of personal cleanliness have risen significantly since then, the same cannot be said about the inner cleanliness of which he speaks. This cleansing, this caring for your inner being is central to the concept of improving yourself and becoming a better person. It needs to be looked after, well maintained and cleansed regularly. How do you do that?

Just like the physical body the answer lies in what you feed it. Good nourishment in other words and oiling too. Greasing the joints of your inner being is carried out by ensuring a steady flow of positive energy over them. Surround yourself with only positive, upbeat people. Immerse yourself in positive activities. Don't allow the sediment of negativity to seep in.

Feed yourself on all the good and helpful things which you can do for other people. The more acts of kindness and generosity you perform then the more your inner being will grow and prosper. You'll be well aware of it. You'll feel healthy and vibrant and looking forward with relish to the day ahead and to the next task of giving which you can perform.

The solution is simple and it's simply in what you do. View life as one huge opportunity to help others. Start off by helping yourself.

That means removing all the clutter and debris from your inner being – the self-doubt, negativity and feelings of inadequacy. Consciously evict them. Replace them with positive energy, good humour and … love! You won't find these last-named stocked at your local pharmacy, drug store, beauty shop or supermarket toiletries department but humour and love are the finest cleansing agent known. The good news is that you possess a limitless supply within you. So raid your inner store and put them to use!

Neither look up to the rich nor down on the poor

When I first read this 'rule' of Carvers I almost burst into spontaneous cheering and applause. Well actually I did! Because I just love when wisdom is expressed simply and pragmatically. When it's an expression you can instantly relate to and just know in your gut that it's right. That it has been told just as it is by someone who knows it, who has been there, seen it, done it. The most profound truths in life are indeed the simplest. You can see the truth in both sides of Carver's assertion all around you.

While I know that most of you would not be seen dead as part of a crowd of screaming, deranged lunatics clamouring from behind a barrier to catch a glimpse of the stars as they make their way along a red-carpeted sidewalk at a glitzy movie premier (you wouldn't would you)? there is certainly a significant amount of people who would – and do!

In the wider sense, a large percentage of people are, whether they know it or not, influenced in many ways by the celebrity culture rife in present day society. There exists a tendency to follow celebrities on social media, hang on their every word and model personas on them.

The reality of course is that, outwith their own spheres of special ability, these celebrities are no better versed in life or important aspects of it than the next man or woman. Yet star-struck suckers listen to them. These 'groupies' forget that, whether buying into the movie show spectacle or into the latest sporting fad or purchasing ridiculously expensive designer goods or whatever, it is the small guy (that's you, not them) who, one way or another, picks up the tab at the end of that day!

They (the public) fall for the trick of a cynical media creating in their minds the illusion that they have a relationship with the star. This is the perception upon which much of popular success relies. While such people are happy to indulge their immature, star-dazzled behaviour blissfully unaware (or perhaps fully aware)! that they are but pawns manipulated, they are often equally befuddled in their approach to the poor and less well off in society.

For my part, I have long been distressed by the plight of homeless people (and I refer to that in the *'Know Your Angels'* section of this book). Personal experience teaches me that it's a horrible situation to be in.

When I see a homeless person, any homeless person, I feel deep compassion for them. I never ask how they came to be in their present situation, that would be critical, judgemental. For me the simple fact that they are without a place to stay and need help is sufficient to warrant my concern and action to assist them.

You can have no way of knowing who these people are, what their lives were like previously, what cause or circumstance brought them to their sorry state ... and neither should you care. Just be sure that it is a fate which can befall anyone. No-one is exempt from disaster or misfortune striking. Everyone needs help somehow or some time in their lives. What a magical opportunity for you to be the person who provides it!

To those who would query the legitimacy of certain poor people begging in the street for example, I simply say that, regardless of how they come to be in that situation, whether self-inflicted or not, the very fact that they feel the need to ask for help in such a way says it all. Can you even begin to imagine how it would feel for you to have to approach a stranger in the street and hold your hand out for a few coppers? Think about it ... visualise it ... it's not pleasant is it?

So what if there are those less than genuine cases, career beggars and those milking your sympathy? Life will catch up with such wrong-doers sooner or later. One way or another, it always does. Karma is a powerful force. By the same token your generosity in helping all who appear to be deserving, without judgement or favour, will reflect well on you. Your inner being will celebrate and be enriched beyond measure!

Lose, if need be, without squealing

Among the celebrities who many in life fawn over and seek to imitate, the sports fraternity is among the most high profile and talked about. Despite my life long interest in sport and the whole ethos surrounding it and those who participate in it, I find myself massively underwhelmed by the majority of today's ludicrously over-paid super stars.

When I refer to their over-payment, I am not one of those who resents what they earn. I believe in capitalism and know that whatever money these sports people are paid will circulate in the economy to the general benefit of all. No, my beef is that the majority of these athletes are not sports people at all as in 'behave in a sporting manner'. I'd go as far as to say that they all, with but a few notable exceptions, know not the first thing about what true sportsmanship is. They sure as heck don't practice it!

What they do appear to practice is cheating. If it's not drugs and corruption outside of play, then it's blatant fouling in play, so-called 'mind games' and a level of professional misconduct that would be totally unacceptable in most other fields of work. It's much more than just a 'win-at-all-costs' attitude. It's psychopathic. And never more so than when they lose!

Then the outpouring of complaints and excuses reaches epidemic proportions. Everyone and everything is to blame but themselves. It's squealing at an epic level. Carver would be appalled, and quite justifiably so.

Apart from a lack of good grace or any empathy with the opponent, the squealing which Carver refers to reveals a deeper fault. It is one rife in modern day society. *It is a reluctance to accept responsibility for oneself and ones own life and actions.*

Today there is a lack of trust. There is a lack of trust because people lack respect for others, the latter being fundamentally due to their own lack of self respect. After all if you don't trust yourself to behave with decency then you're not going to expect to find it in anyone else.

Most people 'hate' politicians. They harbour this deep loathing because politicians are, quite rightly, perceived to be devious, deceitful and lacking in integrity. But in truth, people get exactly the politicians they deserve.

Why? Because politicians come from the same culture and society which they represent. They are exceptionally duplicitous and disingenuous of course but, if people want to demand honesty and integrity from their political representatives then they must first start to behave with honesty and integrity themselves.

The same principle applies with respect to their sports heroes, movie stars or to any other group in the limelight or in society in general.

Today everything is contracts and litigation. Selfishness and greed pervades much of society. Rapacious lawyers and government give it momentum. Politicians interfere in ever more areas of people's lives and the legal profession actively promotes the 'blame game' in liability claim litigation. All around us there is squealing when things don't go our way.

How about lose if need be, but then take a good hard look at yourself. That's where the responsibility, win or lose, lies.

Most significantly, when keeping your mouth shut and examining your own performance or behaviour, you're taking responsibility for your own actions and putting yourself in control of your own destiny.

Win without bragging

I am inclined to believe that the guy who squeals most when he loses is likely also to be the guy who brags most when he wins. The two traits just go together naturally. Both are born from the same tendencies toward over-inflated ego and a lack of any sense of self-responsibility. The term 'self-centred' comes to mind. In this case meaning predominantly selfish.

Yet self-centred can also refer to your self-centre as in your deep inner being. That part of you which is who you are. Your spirit which knows intuitively what is right and wrong, good and bad and when you are doing one or the other. It is the part of you which requires to be nurtured as you have already learned and it needs constant nourishment. There-in is the paradox. Your self centre does require your constant attention and vigilance but you must not behave outwardly in a self-centred way. The latter shows that you care only for yourself and that you care not about the well-being of others.

Of course the way to attend to the needs of your inner being, your self centre, is to do the exact opposite of what a classically self-centred person would do! That is to pay attention to and take care of the needs of others. To put it another way, nourish their self centre by providing for their needs!

When you do the right thing by other people in this way, don't brag about it. Bragging in any context is not attractive. Sure, if you feel that you've done something well or achieved something of merit then there is a natural tendency to want to talk about it. Basking in the glow of your own glory can be a warm sensation – up to a point! But generally it's best not to talk too much of your perceived success. In the first instance some may not see what you're talking about in the same light at all. They might not agree that you did a good job. They might even feel that you did whatever you're talking about rather badly. Even if they do agree that your success was a worthy one, people don't like to hear the actual perpetrator shout too loudly about it.

Leave the complimentary remarks and retelling of your story of success to others. It is far more credible that way anyway. When a second or third party shouts your praises it reflects well on you. That's the exact opposite of the effect of bragging.

Oh! … and your inner self does not like to hear you brag. It makes your spirit feel bad and thereby detracts from any good that your action created.

Always be considerate of women, children and older people

This is a noble ideal and self-explanatory, isn't it? It could well be modified to read *"Always be considerate to everyone but particularly so to the weak and under-privileged!"* I suspect that you all readily agree with the sentiment expressed and sometimes enact it. Maybe not as often as you yourself would like to or feel that you should.

No sweat, if you have not been as conscientious in this department as you might have been, now is a good time to start. It is an attitude that you can practice and improve on.

The first thing is to know the meaning of empathy. Empathy is the ability to understand and share the feelings of another. It is being able to put yourself in someone else's shoes or see things from their perspective. Positioned thus you see yourself in their situation as a fellow participant in what they are experiencing. By taking the focus off yourself in this way you can realise that other people's pains, frustrations and discomforts are as real to them as your own are to you, and often far worse.

Once you can empathise in this way, and fueled by the compassion you are feeling, offer assistance. Most critically - act on it! The best intentions in the world are meaningless unless acted on. All too often you fail on that one simple premise of not turning an intention into an action.

The 'trick' is to perform these acts regularly. Daily is best. They needn't be big things but they do need to be done. Once you start the process of regularly recognising the difficulty some other person is experiencing and doing something about it you will find that, as well as random opportunities to help various people arising, you will develop a rota of regular recipients of your assistance who you will come to know on a deeper level. They in turn will cherish your attentions and the fact that you are always considerate of them.

Be too brave to lie

Bravery is often depicted as a soldier in battle, racing to help a wounded colleague while under fire from all sides, or some similar heroic scenario. And yes, such acts do constitute bravery. Committing them takes incredible courage.

But there are other areas of your life which require you to be brave too - but in different ways.

Among them, and possibly of the greatest importance, is the courage it requires to protect your inner self, your integrity, your truth. Carver has said, "Be too brave to lie." This is sterling advice which reveals great insight into the human spirit on his part. Because when you lie it is yourself you are betraying. You are short changing yourself. You are being less than the person you know yourself capable of being. You are being cowardly.

While it may seem at times easier to lie, the actual truth is that it is not. Don't believe me? Well, have you ever found 'a lie catching up with you'? Have you ever experienced the feeling of relief when, having told the truth, your feared expectations of dire consequences failed to materialise? I'll bet that your answer to both those questions is "Yes!" There is your proof. Lying may appear at face value to be an easier option but your real life experience strongly indicates otherwise.

Then there is the question of integrity. Do you ever consider integrity, your integrity? You should. Because your integrity is part of your deepest, inner being. It is the quality of being honest and having strong moral principles. It is your most valued asset. You cannot put a price on it. Yet many people sell it cheaply. And they do so when they lie.

Your integrity once thus compromised is difficult, if not impossible, to retrieve. It is as if a part of you has been ripped out and then used as a public football. You chase after it endlessly but it's always kicked out of your reach. The 'players' are aware it is your integrity they are playing with but won't return it. They prefer to know you as a liar, someone untrustworthy. That suits them also because it allows them to feel superior and draws attention from their own imperfections – but that's another matter.

Worst of all, you come to see yourself in the same ignominious light. You become a dishonourable person to yourself. You feel contemptible, negative and pessimistic and you see others in the same cynical way. It really is a downward spiral and a not at all happy way to live your life.

So don't lie. The benefits of telling the truth far outweigh the consequences of being untruthful. Becoming a better person demands that you protect your integrity. Only when you take full responsibility for everything that you say and do in life can you truly be free to grow and prosper. That requires that you be too brave to lie.

Be too generous to cheat

Under the heading 'Lose if need be without squealing' I referred to present day sports stars for whom the practice of cheating is second nature. Deliberately flouting the rules is endemic in sport. Yet in many ways what we see happening on the sports field is but a reflection of wider society. It is just that the nature of sports and the people who participate make them highly visible. What they do is seen in the stadiums and more so on television. Their actions are recorded, replayed and discussed at length in the media, the workplace and the pub. Their errant behaviour is subject to microscopic examination.

Cheating in general society is no less prevalent than is the case in sports, it's just not broadcast live on national television! All those bemoaning the lack of integrity among their sporting heroes benefit from the fact that the focus on the short-comings of celebrities draws attention away from their own imperfections.

Those reluctant to play by the rules in life shouldn't really be surprised when footballers or athletes or racing drivers don't play by the rules when in competition. *After all if you're not prepared to behave with decency yourself then you shouldn't expect to find it in anyone else.*

Cheating is ubiquitous. You find it in sport, in major banks and businesses and in politics. From the highest earners in industry and commerce to the Cockney barrow boy flogging a dodgy watch at the Sunday market. Everyone cheats.

Yet behavioural psychologists tell us that humans have an innate disposition not to cheat! This they say is a survival trait based on the life and death needs of prehistoric, group-dwelling hunter-gatherers. But people today increasingly discard this basic instinct. Why?

There are those who strongly believe in the privilege of being part of a community and who want to respect rules and meet their obligations - but there is a change in society which has driven the growth of cheating. Social sanctions against cheating are becoming ever harder to implement as society disintegrates in the face of individual freedom being considered the priority, more so than the community or even family. When cheating reaches a certain profusion it becomes impossible to contain. Rules are there to be broken. Meeting ones obligations under the rules is for somebody else. Almost nobody gets found out and when they do the penalties are trivial.

Which brings me back to my example of sports stars. They can behave with impunity precisely because the penalties are pathetic. What is two weeks wages in a fine to a player earning millions of dollars a year? They don't give a hoot what supporters, the ordinary man in the street or the general public think. They can behave disgracefully without consequences and they don't need your approval! If our sports stars, business leaders, politicians and celebrities can act with such dishonesty and disdain without fear of any repercussion then the rest follow their example. Cheating becomes the norm. People feel no shame. They should.

Because if they valued their integrity they would know that no amount of money on earth could buy it. They'd know that the benefits of being honest, chivalrous even (yes that old word), kind and generous to others far outweigh any monetary gain or rise in (perceived) status to be gained from cheating. They'd know that doing what they do is easy, anyone can do that. But it takes conviction and resolve to have principles, live by them and enact them daily when the general trend is to do the exact opposite.

When you refuse to cheat you are also being generous. You are permitting the other guy to interact with you knowing that you will adhere to the rules. You are giving him the same chance that you expect to be granted to you. You are treating him with respect

It takes extreme courage to stand by your principles and act with integrity while all around you are not doing so. Carver recognised this. But he was also a pragmatist. He believed in practical solutions. He knew that by refusing to cheat he would always win!

Take your share of the world and let others take theirs

Every living creature, be it wild animal or human being, is entitled to its space on this planet ... there are just those whose space I don't want to be within a million miles of mine!

But just because I am not comfortable around certain people (in-laws come to mind)! does not mean that I do not respect their right to be who they are and to live their lives in the same peace and harmony which I want for myself. The key word here is 'respect'. Add to that 'empathy'.

Knowing and understanding that another person has the same core feelings and needs as yourself allows you to appreciate that they too have aspirations, dreams, things that they want and need in their life. They have ways they want to live their life. They too need their space, their air to breathe and their ways of enacting their life. While their space and air may be somewhat different to what you aspire to, they are entitled to them. And you yourself are fully entitled to your space. So do not be afraid to claim it and to occupy it.

Remember that, if you wish others to think well of you, then you must first think well of yourself. If you want others to value you as a person then you must first value yourself. You must comprehend that you have just the same right to your place on the planet and to be heard as does any other person. Exercise your right and allow others to do likewise. When you act with integrity, courage, kindness and humour others will recognise the confidence in you and afford you the space that you merit.

POWER POINT - *"Act with integrity, courage, kindness and humour and others will recognise your strength and afford you respect."*

Whether you feel that you wish to follow Carver's eight cardinal virtues to the letter (and why wouldn't you)? or not, the first things that you must have clearly defined in your conscious mind are just what are your core convictions. What are the principles which you wish to form the whole basis of your being? How do you intend to define and assert your integrity?

People that you admire are a good source of inspiration and motivation in this department. Who-ever you choose to model yourself on, it is highly likely that that person was very good at living out what they believed in and could be relied on to do the right thing at the right moment. This is what you must do also.

Don't think in terms of monumental achievements, that is not practical. Rather act out in small ways, and day by day, consistently, your core convictions. First you must know just what those are.

If you haven't a firm destination in mind and plotted your course accordingly then you're destined to meander aimlessly. How can you be stable and resolute if you don't know where you're going or if you repeatedly change your intended destination? Of course you can't. So do a 'Carver'!

* Think through what your core convictions are or what you want them to be.

* When you are absolutely rock solid sure of what they are, write them down.

* Place the list where you can see it daily.

* Deliberately refer to it daily.

* Repeat aloud to yourself several times each day the core convictions on your list.

* Say "I am … " living the conviction. For example, "I am too brave to lie."

By defining your operating principles for your life in this way, impressing them on your subconscious by writing them down and then following the repetitive actions stated, you will cement your core convictions in your inner being. They will become you and you will be them.

You can do no better than to choose and to implement as your core convictions, Carver's Eight Cardinal Virtues!

Chapter 18

ALL IN THE MIND

You have set yourself a goal, persevered doggedly with your endeavours and arrived at your desired outcome. You've achieved success – right? Wrong!

Because, contrary to what you may have heard or learned elsewhere, real success is a state of mind not to be mistaken with material gain nor a specific achievement. If you are totally focused on a particular goal and have labeled your arrival there as 'success', then you've set yourself up for a big disappointment.

Yes, there will quite rightly be a moment of elation at the point of completion ... but wait ... you now must set another goal and strive all over again! I'm reminded of the guy who, having worked and saved for years to be able to afford the house of his dreams, eventually buys it and moves in. Then almost straight away starts to yearn for a 'bigger, better' one. Not realising that, regardless of how often he moves house, he will never feel truly satisfied.

So success in the context of achieving a goal is but momentary. It is a fleeting emotion to be followed by no such feeling until, hopefully, the satisfactory conclusion of the next project.

Now there's nothing wrong with material gain and wanting to move on to the next goal. Indeed, you must set such targets throughout your life. They are your purpose. But don't think of achieving the goal as 'the time when you will be successful and happy'. What you need is to be able to experience those emotions of success and joy all the time ... and starting now!

To enjoy your endeavours to the full you must feel successful while doing them. That means at all times, every minute, every day throughout. Not just for a brief interlude at their conclusion. With the best will in the world, not all undertakings conclude 'successfully'. In those instances there'd be no enjoyment of success at all!

Success, and especially with regard to leading a good life, cannot be only about the completion of an endeavour. It has to be about the endeavour itself, the journey. In becoming a better person, in improving yourself, it is critical to understand this fundamental truth, otherwise you risk being locked into a lifetime of stress, frustration and lack of self worth. Of never feeling successful!

POWER POINT - *"Leading a good life is about enjoying the journey!"*

How can you enjoy the sensation of success if it is limited to just a few moments at isolated periods in time? To be fully functional, thrive and prosper you need to be able to live success constantly.

Remember that authentic success is a sense of satisfaction and fulfillment which you experience minute by minute, day by day, every moment of your life. You can achieve this in two ways :

(1) Clear out your physical, mental and emotional clutter.

a. This means achieving a physical condition and indulging in a healthy diet, both of which please you, which you feel at ease with and which adds to your self-confidence.

b. Plus you should work at thinking clearly and simply. This will usually involve a process of uneducation, removing from your mind many well entrenched beliefs and thought processes placed there from early childhood and then through schooling, peer pressure and culture.

c. And ridding yourself of emotional clutter will require a close examination of all your relationships, unresolved issues within them and dealing with them decisively. Completely eradicate from your life all negative people, even family and former friends.

(2) Engage with and empower others.

Give generously of your time and effort to help others get what they want. If their want is to feel better about themselves, to self improve generally or in a specific area of their life, then help them get there. You will find that the biggest beneficiary of your kindness will be you! You'll first experience spiritual wealth then through that an inward calm and increased confidence. You will feel successful!

Find success within yourself and in the joy you bring to others. Work at being a successful, caring human being. Remind yourself daily that you are successful. Understand that success is a state of mind.

~

Once you accept that certain aspects of your life are fixed and have to be accepted, you will stop fighting against them. It will not be a surrender. It will give you the energy you need for the battles that still have to be won.

It's inevitable, for example, that sadness will overtake you from time to time. Guess what? There's nothing wrong with being sad. Just like all our other emotions it exists for a reason. Live the experience, see it through. The sadness is allowing you to grieve and to heal. Those who say, "Cheer up," or offer some other equally asinine comment are urging you to fight against your natural feelings. That's not healthy.

There will also be times in your life when you are happy and contented. When that is so, accept it. Don't ask how did this situation come about? or why me? Just accept it and enjoy it. Life, real life, really is that simple!

One of the most important thing to remember is that you are not perfect. There's no point trying to be. You can however try to be better than you are. In fact your aim should be to be a better you today than you were yesterday. Setting that as your goal is realistic. It will lead to continual improvement in whatever areas of your life you have set out to enhance.

Get comfortable too with the idea that sometimes less is better. Today's world of internet, smart phones and instant contact technology may well have brought knowledge to the finger tips of the world but do you really need to know absolutely everything, about everybody and every situation? ... and do you need to know it **now**?

Even before the age of senseless internet chatter the smart ones in any area of life learned that less is more and that quality counts. Such people don't follow the herd. They keep a low profile and lead quiet, uncluttered lives. They are content.

For you, don't be afraid to be a contrarian. What's a contrarian? A contrarian is a person who opposes or rejects popular opinion. Not just for the sake of it but because they have reasoned out their viewpoint for themselves. As the popular view expressed by society at large is almost certain to be one which is unlikely to get you ahead in your pursuit of excellence in whatever it is that you're doing, then it is actually necessary that you oppose it.

After all, only a very small percentage of people achieve exceptional goals. It follows that only this select group have the 'right' attitude in this context. Therefore it also follows that everyone else's attitude in this context is the 'wrong' attitude.

It is essential therefore not to automatically go with the opinions and ideas of the bulk of the population, as espoused daily on television, in the pub and in the workplace. Their views are liable to be worthless with regard to what you have set out to achieve and the ways in which you intend to achieve it. They may make up the majority of opinion but it is 'unsuccessful' opinion!

Rather look to what exceptional people are doing. There's a lot less of them but they'll be doing things differently from the average person. They therefore are contrarians. You should be too.

Erna Dewachter is a contrarian. Don't rack your brain, you will not have heard of her. She is neither famous nor wealthy, at least not in monetary terms. Yet she is the very epitomé of an independent thinker (see chapter of same title) as in one who has full control of her life and all in it. She doesn't run with the herd.

Erna is respected and shunned in equal measure precisely because she expresses herself simply and clearly and conducts her life likewise. No-one is left uncertain as to who she is or what she is about. Erna is her own woman, proud of it and lives life strictly on her terms. She is very much the perfect example of a confident, self-determined being, living her life with integrity, joyful in what she does. She is deeply happy.

To some their day revolves around established schedules, clocks and timetables. To Erna her only agenda is the call of her land. It is in working in the field, in the open air and concentrating her time and attention on her substantial acreage of trees, plants, flowers and vegetables (and she is self sufficient in fruit and veg) that she finds her truth and intuition in life. She has created - not found - true contentment. This hard work and love for what she does is the driving force of her existence. She laughs a lot and radiates her self-assurance and even humour outwards on all around her.

Like Erna, aim to live life at your pace. Only do that in life which you enjoy. Never concern yourself with how much you can do in a set time or with 'running behind'. I learned long since to employ a 'do what I can do' attitude. I don't practice schedules nor expect it from others. I recommend that you drop them. It's one of my great 'secrets' but I concede that few will follow me … yet it's what is truly profitable.

I'm the guy whose phone is often switched off and when on I rarely answer it. I rush no-where and answer to no-one. It's called freedom. Don't be fooled. It's also seriously profitable in every meaning of the term.

The trick however is not one of doing nothing, far from it. But when choosing to do something do it only if :

It's great fun

A high pay off activity (spiritually or materially)

You do it with excellence

and

Don't concern yourself with anything else – at all – ever!

When you follow those simple rules you will be behaving differently from the majority of people. You will be a contrarian. You will be one capable of achieving exceptional goals and of realising your true value in life.

The Road To Joyful Living!

PART 7

Valuation

in which you examine your true worth

Joseph T.Riach

Chapter 19

THE INDEPENDENT THINKER

The Independent Thinker awakened from his deep, untroubled sleep at exactly the hour that he had predetermined; just as he had done every day for most of his adult life. He needed no alarm clock nor companion to arouse him. The time at which he wanted to awaken could vary, as indeed could his location or well-being, but every night he slept as long as he intended to and every day he awakened at just the time he wanted to. To achieve this feat he had programmed his subconscious to be his alarm clock and trained himself thus over many years. In practice his technique was simple. Last thing before putting his head down he would say aloud - "I will sleep soundly and untroubled for six hours (or however many) and awaken at seven o'clock (or whatever hour)." In the beginning he had repeated the instruction several times but for a long time past no longer needed to.

Note also that his instruction included the words "soundly and untroubled." This too worked like clockwork. He couldn't remember a time of other than lovely, long, cosy sleeps! This latter feature, sound sleep, was also aided by other aspects of his lifestyle, namely -

- Regular exercise and fresh air

- Varied and healthy Mediterranean diet

- Worry and stress free living

These last three mentioned required strong self discipline. The

Independent Thinker had that in bucket loads having worked on it since youth. It was in some ways a contradiction because he hated routine. So he varied his routine from moment to moment, day to day. This kept him unpredictable to others and alert.

On this particular day after getting up, the first thing he did was his exercise – at least an hour of high intensity work – and then his meditation and mantras (more about that elsewhere). With his physical and spiritual training attended to, the rest of the morning was reserved for work (for him a thoroughly enjoyable activity). Lunchtime onwards was for relaxation, fun and assisting some less fortunate folks. The latter might sound altruistic but The Independent Thinker found the activity intellectually and spiritually rewarding. He was getting something out of it too!

There was much more to The Independent Thinker than just the 'trick' of waking up when he wanted to, eating well and keeping his mind, body and blood pressure in check! In reality The Independent Thinker had an itinerary of activities which would appear daunting to most people but he had created a work pattern, relaxed and unhurried, in which he could produce more and better quality art (as he chose to call his work) in one morning than an average person might achieve in one month! In fact a casual observer might have considered him so relaxed as not to be working at all. But his mind was constantly alert, analysing and planning; at least that is until he chose to shut it down, also by subconscious command. With this mindset The Independent Thinker had the self-assurance to be unaffected by conflicts or criticism and neither worry nor stress entered his life because he simply did not permit them.

A central facet of The Independent Thinker's character was that he shunned the limelight. You would never pick him out in a crowd. He preferred the anonymity of the background but, when the limelight did demand, then he would handle that with ease. No, what The Independent Thinker really loved was his work, and even more so a challenge!

Were anyone to have the temerity to suggest to The Independent Thinker that some proposed venture or undertaking was impossible then they'd be best advised to do so from a safe distance and in full combat gear! Working on an 'impossible' project was everything to him, so much so that the actual end game, the achievement of a successful conclusion, left him feeling empty. Hence the need in his life to embark quickly on to the next project and then the next and the next and so on. His imagination you see would not, could not stop. This is why all independent thinkers never retire. How do you retire an active imagination? Why would you stop doing that thing in life which you most enjoy?

POWER POINT - *"How do you retire an active imagination? Why would you stop doing that thing in life which you most enjoy?"*

The Independent Thinker had become successful in life precisely because of his inquisitive mind and his desire to expand and perfect his knowledge. He had made himself a specialist in his field. He had worked purposefully, obstinately and persistently to develop his ideas and visions, usually working alone and often in the face of external opposition. He ignored criticism. It amused him to think that he was regarded as some sort of eccentric simply because -

• He refused to go with the herd – independence and space is his reserve

• He preferred the simple life – sunshine, nature and love of others

- He didn't complain – rather he created what he wanted

- He spoke with integrity and of truth and respect

- He believed in simplicity of thought and action

- He lived life as an authentic participant

- He took the risk of being successful

- He didn't take things personally – 'others views are a reflection of themselves'

- He'd speak little of his affairs and then only to those few who empathised

- He didn't read newspapers - 'their content is half lies and half garbage'

- He loathed journalists – 'they make it good, make it big and make it up!'

- He hated politicians – same as above but worse

- He kept his mobile switched off – more so in restaurants or when in company

- He communicated clearly - said what he thought and what he meant

- He was courageous – asked for and expressed what he wanted

- He only mixed with positive minded people

- He avoided negative people - even family and former friends

- He didn't waste valuable life time watching third rate

'soaps' and reality TV shows

- He refused to believe everything he was told – he worked it out for himself

- He didn't jump to conclusions - he worked things out for himself

- He had a lively wit and a wicked sense of humour

- He was self critical but never sorry for himself

- He refused to gossip or speak ill of others

- He was self-effacing and generous

- He always did his best

The Independent Thinker completed his day by finishing off the above list which he had prepared for one of his *Wake Up Leisure and Learning Courses** which he was conducting in the morning. He wryly reflected that he could easily have added one hundred and one more traits and life skills to the collection, but those would suffice for now. He closed his laptop, reclined in his lounger on the open terrace and, looking up at a clear, starry sky of wondrous beauty he allowed himself a contented smile. Then he unburdened all his current work, thoughts and plans to his subconscious and 'switched off.'

Stretching out on his bed he closed his eyes and whispered, "I will sleep soundly and untroubled for .... "

~

Do you have what it takes to be an independent thinker? How many of the following adjectives apply to you?

Adventurous, analytical, assured.

Demanding, dogged, hard-working.

Honest, independent, intellectual.

Introverted, inventive, logical.

Multi-faceted, non-conformist, planning.

Quiet, quirky, rational, reserved, resolute.

Self-confident, self-critical, structured.

Theoretical, unsociable, visionary, witty.

* Wake Up Leisure and Learning Breaks – Personal Mentoring and Business Guidance courses run by the author in southern Portugal. Information at https://www.tomriach.com/wakeup

Chapter 20

WHAT'S YOUR CHOICE?

Two workmates who do the same job in the same factory for the same wages are talking in the pub one Friday evening after work. Annual holidays is the theme of the conversation.

Joe Slagg is bemoaning the fact that he cannot afford a holiday away from home and will have to stay with 'er indoors (his spouse) and the 'screaming kids' for the fortnight. He lights up yet another fag from the still smouldering tabby of his previous one and weeps into his thirteenth pint of beer. The beer is the last one he can 'afford' but somehow he'll be back tomorrow for another gutfull as he has done every night of the year for the past fifteen years.

Frank Lovejoy on the other hand enthuses as to how he's looking forward to his Caribbean cruise with his wife and family.

"How the hell can you afford that on our wages?" bleeds Joe.

"Easy," chirps Frank, "I only come here once a month!"

Then, "Oh, I must be going. I've to pick up my Merc from it's service before closing. Can't be late home, it's steak, scallops and champagne for dinner tonight. Aren't I lucky?"

Then he was off.

Frank you see, understood that we each have a choice as to how we spend not just our cash but our time, our lives. That we owe it to ourselves and to our loved ones to make the most of every precious second.

POWER POINT - *"Your duty to yourself and to those who matter in your life is to cherish every moment of life and spend it wisely."*

What's your choice?

~

For much of my life I was a great believer in the benefits of owning property, particularly my own home. In more recent times I've become less convinced that it is necessary to do so. There are a number of reasons for my gradual change of heart on the matter. They range from a simple 'because it is just the way I feel' attitude to an altogether more profound, and therefore significant rationale.

In the first instance I've never been entirely comfortable with the notion that my home is also my main investment. Yet I readily concede that the vast majority of people do live happily with this reality. It's a reasonably sound concept. Also it's the fashion. Who wouldn't want to own their own home?

Well those who don't want to feed a mortgage (home loan) for a start!

I've been one of those party to a mortgage loan and I've been a promoter of them too, so I know a thing or two about them. In line with my general belief that borrowing money, other than for a sound business proposition, is not a good practice, I likewise feel that you should not get into debt in order to buy a house. If you can buy it outright 'cash down' without the need to borrow then that's a quite different matter. Yet, even given that premise, I've come to the conclusion that owning my own home is not necessary. I prefer to rent.

What! am I mad? Yes, quite possibly, but not for the reason that

I would choose renting a property to live in over the option of buying it! By renting I may be feeding a greedy landlord's profits it's true, but then again I may be providing vital income for a hard up widow. It depends on your perspective. Anyway, in all your dealings you should seek out value and circumstances where you are helping others.

POWER POINT - *"Look for value in all that you do and circumstances where you are helping others."*

When you rent a property, rent from an individual of integrity. One to whom your support is important and appreciated. Then you are holding true to your ideals of life as a servant and of creating joy in the lives of both yourself and another. You are also creating flexibility in terms of where you live and when!

In renting you are benefiting from not being tied for long periods to any one property or location. This is particularly significant in the current age of home businesses, self-employment and internet related work. Much has been made of the fact that, by working remotely and without any need to daily commute or report to a place of work, anyone can work anywhere anytime. In other words you can live where-ever you choose in your own town or country, or indeed anywhere in the world. Not owning property makes switching locations at the drop of a hat just that so much easier. Guess what? I like easy.

Easy includes not being subject to the responsibilities of ownership. Nor indeed having your name appear on deeds, public records or contracts of any kind when it can possibly be avoided. It comes under the heading of 'keeping a low profile', of not being ostentatious. And why not?

Having a high public profile is not a necessary requisite of leading a caring and generous life, of being a better person. Even some hugely 'successful personalities' do not put themselves consistently in the public eye. Many maintain a low profile and are effectively invisible to the outside world. These last are probably the smarter ones. They let others bask in the limelight but stay themselves well below the parapet. Not being in the 'firing line' gives them a big advantage in being able to lead a quiet life of service to others. With many their anonymity does indeed extend to not having debt, not owning property nor cars and, in fact, not having their name appear on documents nor anywhere. They are almost invisible and as such able to pursue much more effectively their chosen life as servants to the needy and the world at large.

My definitive reason for feeling that it is neither necessary nor desirable for you to own your own property is altogether more profound. It lies at the very heart of your perception of yourself and of how you wish to live your life as a better and more caring person. It's all to do with how you define your role in life.

Some years ago I purchased a property (cash, no loan) in the Georgian New Town area of Edinburgh. It dated from the year eighteen-twenty. Although it had been occupied it was run down and in a bad state of repair. My intention was to utilise the building as both a residence and a business premise.

With all proper planning consents and building warrants in place, I set about implementing the not inconsiderable building works and renovations. The plan was to return the property, inside and out, to it's former period magnificence. This ambition was in due course realised. I was very proud of the completed renovation and felt privileged both to have had the opportunity to be instrumental in the undertaking and to have occupancy of such a fine dwelling.

Shortly after completion of the project I received a letter from a near neighbour. In their note they took exception to the fact that the property was now partially a business premise and that a sign proclaiming the fact had been erected outside.

This, the writer claimed, detracted from the character of the neighbourhood and devalued it. Some reference too was made to property developers who rode rough shod over planning laws and desecrated sites of historical beauty and the rights of those living there ... or some words to that effect. The sort of disjointed, angry rhetoric I would normally ignore. Except this time I didn't.

I penned a polite reply in which I pointed out that, in purchasing the property, I had accepted responsibility for it, its origins and its history. I explained that I had exercised my responsibility with care and diligence. I had reproduced in fine detail, both inside and out, the original character of the building; so that not just myself, but present and future generations could enjoy its grandeur.

I wrote that, far from owning the building, I saw myself simply as its temporary custodian, nothing more; and that I took my role of steward seriously and would continue to do so. I concluded by inviting the writer to visit and see the magnificently restored interior. (In the event they did visit, admired the entire property and we became firm friends).

Now the point I ask you to note is ... *"I saw myself simply as its temporary custodian, nothing more"* and that *"present and future generations could enjoy its grandeur"*. These words represented exactly how I felt at the time and do so even more so now. I have come to realise that the so-called owner of a property, any property, is nothing more than a temporary custodian. That being the case, what is the point in owning it? You can still enjoy all it has to offer and tend and care for it lovingly as a tenant. In due time that privilege and responsibility will pass on to someone else.

In the meantime you can contemplate my assertion that there is, strictly speaking, no such thing as a personal possession. Any material object is but something that you have the temporary use of and are therefore temporarily responsible for. Whatever you 'own' will pass away or pass on to someone else at some point.

My feeling therefore is that there is no purpose in getting bogged down with the pursuit of material possessions, properties or otherwise. Better by far to put whatever material wealth you may have to work for the greater good.

It has been asked, "Which is better, to be seriously wealthy and to suffer the burden of having to care for it or to realise that wealth is as much of a hindrance as anything?" When you come to see that the second part of that statement can often represent the wiser option then, regardless of your wealth, you can choose to put such material wealth as you have, as well as your own time and energy, into the daily provision of kindness and charity to others.

POWER POINT - *"Put your time and energy into the daily provision of kindness and charity to others."*

There are those who live in fine homes or villas (with or without a mortgage) who are poorer by far in spiritual life terms than many of the homeless and destitute. This because they have made the accumulation of material wealth the entire focus of their lives. Don't fall into that trap. Neither choose to be homeless though. Don't subscribe to either of these groups!

Think happiness and abundance by all means. That's fine. Create for yourself and your loved ones a bright and wonderful life. Then enhance it even more by helping others to enjoy a wonderful life too.

That is when you will own much more than anything as insignificant as a mere property. You will own your own life.

Joseph T.Riach

Chapter 21

WHAT'S YOUR VALUE?

A re you a 'Live and Let Die' or a 'Give and Get By' kind of guy? Let's find out.

You are the owner of substantial wealth, built up over many years through hard work and dedication. Do you :

* Keep your wealth to yourself, spending lavishly and leading a jet set party life style? (Live and Let Die)

or

* Distribute substantial amounts to worthwhile causes, charities and the disadvantaged, retaining just enough money for yourself on which to live modestly? (Give and Get By)

There's no right or wrong answer to the above.. At first glance, the second option does appear to be the more morally correct. But is it?

The 'Live and Let Die' guy through his extravagant spending is spreading wealth into the economy, feeding businesses, creating employment, incurring tax. It's the law of abundance at work. The wealth he has created in turn helps drive the economy.

'Give and Get By' is however also stoking the economy. He chooses to relinquish control of his money by giving most of it away but after that the charities or other entities in receipt of his donations employ staff and incur expenditures. So that money too circulates.

Apart from how the money is at outset directed by the respective individuals, in both cases the cash ends up in general circulation and benefiting all. 'Give and Get By' will justifiably feel good about directly assisting worthy causes. But 'Live and Let Die' will know that he is also feeding the masses, so can be quietly satisfied too.

Of course there's the question of preferred life style. Each to his own. One with modest tastes and needs may quite well feel they have no use for lots of money and prefer that someone else has the responsibility of dispensing of it; while a flamboyant personality will be more than happy to splash the cash ... and be seen doing it!

What is undeniable is that those who work with dedication and persevere over many years to accumulate wealth have the right to choose in just what way they dispose of it. They can derive satisfaction from the knowledge that their endeavours ultimately influence the livelihood and well-being of countless others. Directly or indirectly, their achievements benefit all.

As for the moral high ground ... 'Live and Let Die' may appear less caring and 'Give and Get By' may want to be seen to be caring ... but minds and motives are rarely straightforward.

More ...

Of course you may find in addressing my, "Are you a live and let die or are you a give and get by kind of guy?" question that you feel unable to answer clearly one way or another. You may feel that you are a bit of each ... or a bit of neither! This is actually quite normal.

Before looking at that a little more closely I will first state that 'successful' people in life generally have a clear idea of who they themselves are. They therefore have a firm opinion one way or the other regarding this, or any other, topic. Such types are quietly self-confident and sure of who they are (but not brash nor cocky). They will be assertive (not aggressive) and will hold firm views and opinions which they are happy to express with calm authority. They will not be 'fluffy' in what they say, indecisive in action nor unsure about themselves.

Having said that, they like you and everyone else, are constantly seeking balance in their lives and to balance aspects of their personality.

Think of life like learning to ice skate. In the beginning you find it impossible to stay on your feet at all. As you progress you manage to stay upright for longer and longer periods and to move forward ever more surely. In due course and after many false starts, bumps, bruises and much wounded pride, you at last are able to glide around the rink with grace and speed. Once you've learned how to accomplish the skill then you never forget.

Working your way through life and establishing your identity, your *'Who You Are'*, is just the same.

You'll almost certainly have childhood recollections which have instilled in you the, *"My children will never experience that"* attitude. You'll then have proceeded to protect your own children from 'that kind of experience' while unwittingly exposing them to some equally 'rough experience' at another point in spectrum. The effect being that they ultimately fared and developed no better than you in that respect. The experience you created for them, just like yours, lacked equilibrium. It wasn't a balanced experience.

While life is rarely perfectly balanced, those individuals successful in the art of living have established, better than most others, a state of equilibrium. They enjoy a balanced life.

You of course can enjoy a reasonably balanced life too. It may be necessary for you to experience extremes in order to get there.

You may, for example, need to live with both poverty and wealth in order to comprehend the true character of material well-being and from that the ability to integrate both comfortably into your life. You will almost certainly experience the great joys as well as the harrowing sadness of life before arriving at a harmonious understanding of your existence.

You will have achieved such a state when you can, among other things :

* Assert your personality and empathise

* Comfortably rest and play

* Eat and drink well and diet too

* Embrace both nature and technology

* Give generously but not spend recklessly

* Love yourself and others unconditionally

* Have an open heart and even temper

* Think logically and intuitively

* Nurture and protect

* Be gentle and firm

* Be creative and active

* Be determined and relaxed

* Be understanding and empowering

* Be your own person

This last state, being your own person, implies that you know your own mind and that you possess the maturity and calm self-assurance to express yourself freely both in word and in deed. It is generally the mark of one already arrived at a place and time in their life of inner peace and tranquility consistent with achieving good balance.

This is not to diminish in any way your prevalent personality and your outer character which defines you to the world as the individual that you are. That stays intact.

Your response to the, "Are you a live and let die or are you a give and get by kind of guy?" question may depend on whether or not you have accumulated substantial wealth at any point in your life and whether or not you've experienced financial hardship. Then again it may not.

But the degree of exposure to these extremes of wealth that you have experienced will inevitably influence your perception of the power of money and how best to use it.

When you have money you possess the ability to positively influence your life and the people and circumstances in it, in ways not possible when you have none.

Firstly money gives you choices. Put simply, an individual of low wealth might for instance only be able to afford to eat at a down town café whereas a more wealthy person could choose to eat at an upmarket restaurant or at the down town café. The prosperous person might even choose the down market café but critically they have the choice.

Secondly, money is power. The mere fact that you have it can open many doors and alter the way in which others perceive you. Just think of the difference in the demeanour of others towards you when they believe you to have wealth as opposed to their attitude when they know you have none. Consider too your own behaviour towards others in these respects. Possession of money affords you control of your circumstances in your life.

Spending it gives away that power. It is absolutely crucial to understand the simple fact that the real power of money lies in having it ... not spending it. After all, the 'choice' and 'power' which possession of money brings means that you can achieve and possess anything and everything material which you might ever desire – and often without spending any money!

POWER POINT - *"The power of money is in having it, not spending it."*

When you make money – hold on to it! Try to go through one whole day without spending a single cent. When you succeed, and it won't prove easy, try two consecutive days, then three and so on. You'll be surprised at how much spending you can eliminate when you really try. Most people rarely try this. They'd never think to.

Also apply the practice to bigger spending. See what big ticket items you really can eliminate from your expenditure when you truly apply yourself to the task. There are so many things that people consider necessary but which in reality are not. (Do you need twin ovens in the kitchen? Or the latest, most expensive smart phone)? Concentrate any 'spending' instead only in areas that give you a higher return (more money back) than what you've spent. In this case you're not really spending anything at all. You are making money!

Work at concentrating your brain, your subconscious especially, on your personal money management. On ways of only spending on bare necessities and on things which will earn you more money in return. When you do change your attitude and mindset in this way, thinking and acting very simply and very clearly, then you will feel completely at ease with yourself and in control. You will cease to be a victim of the consumer society and experiencing the stress and trauma which it delivers, instead enjoying the freedom and tranquility of one who understands and uses to advantage the power of money.

Having money does not of course make you a better person but it does create opportunities for you to become a better person. It also means that you are not burdened by the low self-esteem and stress often caused by financial shortage and debt.

~

Visitor's to my hugely wealthy client's business premises in an out of town industrial estate were often met by a slightly scruffy individual tinkering with machinery in the yard. When they asked of this character as to where they could find the boss he would inevitably direct them to one of the portakabin offices stacked up inside the workshop. There, the response of an always amused receptionist to the visitors' repeated request to speak with the boss was, "You just spoke to him in the yard!"

On one famous occasion when a bevvy of pin-stripe suited executives arrived from 'the city' to discuss buying my client's business, the 'odd job man', covered in grease and muttering profanities, redirected them to the nearby Holiday Inn. There the 'the boss' would meet them and discuss the deal over lunch. Picture their amazement when on arrival there they were led to a table where waiting for them was seated the self-same labourer … and he was on first name terms with the maitre d'!

Later that afternoon the city boys made my client an offer of several million to buy his business. He turned them down flat. Later he confided to me, "What would I do with all that money? I love my work … and … if my business is worth all that money to them, then it must be worth a heck of a lot more to me!"

My client you see was not only self-effacing and possessing of a mischievous sense of humour, he was also a man fully aware of his own value.

He and those like him who understand their own worth as individuals, not only do not lose out in financial dealings but tend also to be 'winners' in other areas of life. They will generally be well thought of and looked up to in society.

This is because, if you wish others to think well of you then you must first think well of yourself. If you want others to value you as a person then you must first value yourself. You must comprehend that you have just the same right to your place on the planet and to be heard as does any other person.

Applying a monetary value to yourself or your business is not about reducing yourself to the status of a commodity. You are much more important than that. What it does is provide a barometer reading of how well you are doing in life, how well you think of yourself.

One opportunity to properly evaluate your own worth and which will arise at least once in your lifetime is when you apply for employment and write a CV. As a self-employed person and running my own businesses for my entire working life, I've had little need to produce CVs. But many hundreds have crossed my desk over the years and I have had to write my own personal as well as business background reports to accompany project applications and tenders. So a CV or personal history document is always an important one.

A memorable piece of wisdom imparted to me many years since by a mentor older and wiser by far than I, went thus :

"When you write your CV it is the one opportunity you will have in life to be perfect! Don't waste it."

Wonderful advice! However, I would add to that - but never claim what you can't deliver. As my mother would often insist - *"Speak up for yourself ... and then always be true to your word!"*

A young man attended a job interview. Among other things he was asked how much he expected to be paid for the work in question. Wanting to improve on his current earnings but not wishing to price himself out of the market, he quoted a figure which was twenty-five percent greater than his then present salary.

In due course he was awarded the new job and was cock-a-hoop at having won himself such a significant increase in earnings. Meeting with his new employer he expressed his excitement with the work opportunity afforded him and his satisfaction with the wage negotiated. "Me too", revealed his new employer, "I was prepared to pay you twice as much as that!"

The young man you see, had yet to learn to value himself sufficiently. He still saw himself as of lesser worth than his new employer's valuation of him. None-the-less, in asking for the increased salary he had indeed raised his evaluation of his self-worth. That was a start but he had yet some distance to go in understanding and asserting his true value in the world.

The very best way for you to increase your self worth right now, today, is not by writing a sensational job application nor by asking an employer to pay you more - you can of course do that and that's fine! No, what you must do is find someone at a low ebb in life. Someone whose self-esteem needs a boost. Help them to develop the self-confidence to think of themselves, to value themselves, more highly.

When you assist others in this way then the greatest beneficiary of your efforts will be ... you! This is the surest route to becoming aware of your own true value and your place in life.

The Road To Joyful Living!

PART 8

Determination

in which you challenge yourself

Joseph T.Riach

Chapter 22

I'LL SHOW THEM!

S elf-improvement is a purely personal thing. It is not necessary to share it. In fact it's not at all desireable to share it. Apart from the simple fact that it is private, very private, there are two other reasons to keep it to yourself.

One is that sharing with others what you are doing can undo the goodness of your intention. It turns your work on yourself more into a *'look at me'* and *'how good am I'* activity rather than the intimate inner endeavour which it should be.

Secondly, if you do share or if others discover what it is you are about, you will inevitably invite in the critics, doubters and naysayers with their plethora of negative comments and energy sapping ridiculing of your work. So keep your intents to yourself.

Should it happen that others become aware of the fact that you are working to become a better person and they deride what it is that you are trying to achieve then you must not allow the negative vibes with which they bombard you to get to you. You must not allow their mindless envy (for that is what it is) to penetrate your cloak of determination. Rather deflect their negative energy and throw it back on them by adopting an inner, *"I'll show them!"* attitude.

Where others do not know of or ridicule your efforts it can be a good motivator anyway to create an imaginary foe; someone to compete against in order to strengthen your resolve. Even if, as is the case, the opponent is simply yourself!

In this scenario use, *"I'll show them!"* as a mantra to repeat continuously, both to yourself inwardly and said out loud several times each day.

The object of a mantra is to imbue your subconscious with positive thoughts which, in time, will become part of your inner core being. That is, they will replace the negativity, fear and self doubt instilled in you to a greater or lesser degree from birth and through your formative childhood years. I have a couple of favourites which I use most often.

As a lifelong athlete it is not surprising that both are adaptions from the script of the academy award winning "Chariots of Fire" film, the superbly inspirational story of human endeavour and triumph over ones inner self.

My mantras state - *"Today I am running like the wind. Let the world watch in awe and wonder!"*

And - *"Today I'm taking them all on and I'm running them off their feet!"*

(And I do in fact recite these while out running. Blending such mental exercise into a work-out is very effective in making the message stick. You also need not set aside separate time for reciting them later).

By repeating your mantras aloud every day, at least one hundred times each, you implant in your subconscious ever more belief in the truth of what they state. In due course what they state does become fact. They become you. Concentrate on your mantras and watch your performances at work and at play get better and better every day.

"Every day, in every way, I'm getting better and better!"

If the idea of having an opponent (imaginary or otherwise) with whom you are competing works for you and helps to motivate you in your self-improvement work then by all means use the, *"I'll show them!"* approach. Employ the power of competition.

Never lose sight of the fact that the competition is yourself. Every day, little by little, your aim is to improve yourself, your own performance as a human being. Your goal is not to be better than anyone else. Your goal each day is to be a better you than you were yesterday!

POWER POINT - *"Your goal is to be a better you today than you were yesterday."*

Take a look around you and you will find all kinds of successful people. Not just those who have made it big financially or in business but a rich assortment of folk from all walks of life. Ordinary people from various backgrounds who have succeeded in achieving their own particular goals.

It could be the seriously disabled guy who has learned to walk; the charity fund raiser who has reached his financial target; the climber who has overcome his fears and conquered his peak; the parents who have struggled to bring up and educate their family.

Or it could simply be YOU – the guy who wanted to be a better person.

The scenarios are endless. Achievement comes in many shapes and forms, spiritual as often as physical.

For all the diversity that exists in defining success, there is one common bond that unites all successful beings regardless of situation, background, trade or profession, pursuit or ambition. That one common bond is ..... the quality of perseverance!

POWER POINT - *"The common bond that unites all successful beings is the quality of perseverance."*

Ray Kroc, who developed the McDonalds restaurant empire said,

"Nothing in the world can take the place of persistence. Talent will not, nothing is more common than unsuccessful men with talent. Genius will not, unrewarded genius is almost a proverb. Education will not, the world is full of educated derelicts. Persistence and determination alone are omnipotent."

Kroc would know. He suffered countless disappointments and failures before overcoming all adversity to establish what became the worlds largest restaurant chain.

He's not alone in respect of enduring hardship and pain en route to success. Try for size these household names, past and present, as further examples of rags-to-riches real life stories. You'll recognise them all :

Harry Lauder : Andrew Carnegie : Walt Disney

Ralph Lauren : Steve Jobs : Henry Ford : J.K.Rowling

Samuel Walton : Oprah Winfrey : Seve Ballesteros

Fame and fortune did not come easily to any of these celebrities. Most came from humble origins and some from situations of desperate poverty. Some, at points in their lives, had to make do with far less than most ordinary people regard as basic and necessary living standards. All had to fight hard to establish themselves.

For instance, among those mentioned who overcame apparently insurmountable difficulties through application of dogged determination and sheer will are instances of :

Suffering depression and suicidal tendencies

Being sent to work in a mill at age 13 years

Wearing clothes made from potato sacks

Living on free meals and hand outs

Being given away for adoption

Being uneducated and dyslexic

Being molested and abused

Chronic hunger

If you think you've got it bad, then think again. If you think that the road ahead is hard and rocky, then think again. And if you think that there's just no way that you can get ahead and fulfill that cherished dream, then think again.

None of the names mentioned were blessed with any faculties different to yours.

All had two hands, two feet and one brain. They also had ***heart!***

Whatever your ambition and however often you get knocked back - ***Pick yourself up, dust yourself off and start all over again!***

Set your sights on achieving great things in your chosen field or pursuit regardless of the obstacles. In fact, many of the names mentioned would tell you that they used those very obstacles and the adversity they endured as their motivation. You can too and you can use their example as your inspiration.

POWER POINT - ***"In adversity you can find motivation. In the example of others you can find inspiration."***

'Self-improvement', and *'achievement'* are what I do. I speak to my clients and guests and I write about *'success'*. Therefore, I

rarely mention *'failure.'* But you shouldn't be afraid of failure. We've all experienced it. In fact, failure is almost a necessary requisite of success. You'll learn more from one day of failure than you will from one year of success.

POWER POINT - *"You'll learn more from one day of failure than you will from one year of success."*

When failure comes - and it will – pay heed to the lessons to be learned - *then pick yourself up, dust yourself off and start all over again!*

Reaching a goal is never easy. If it were easy then everyone would be a super striker!

There is risk involved, of course there is. If there were no risk then everyone would do it! Whenever you set out to achieve great things, to attain success whether materially or spiritually, you have to take a risk. The risk you take however is simply the risk of being successful. Be bold! *Expose yourself to the risk of success!*

POWER POINT - *"The only risk involved when you set out to self-improve, to become a better person, is the risk of success!"*

I believe, indeed I know from personal experience, that all success is based on perseverance. If your goal is self-improvement, then your prime requirement is to be, and to remain, absolutely determined.

To succeed at anything, you first and always need to think in terms of being a better person. That means practicing and persevering at doing all of the things of which I've written in order to improve your self. All success starts with being a better person.

POWER POINT - *"All success flows from first becoming a better person."*

As George Washington Carver famously stated :

"How far you go in life will depend on your being tender with the young, sympathetic with the striving, tolerant of the weak, respectful of the strong and compassionate with the aged. Because some day in life you will have been all of these."

And I would add … *"and have fun with all of them!"*

Now that's self-improvement!

Good luck on your journey.

The Road To Joyful Living!

PART 9

Valediction

in which this road ends and your journey begins

Joseph T.Riach

EPILOGUE

THE PURPOSE OF BEAUTY

Just when you feel that you have driven through the most stunningly enchanting village in the whole wide world, you swing around the next bend on any country road in the Perigord region of south-west France and there before you is another village even more entrancing. After that one there's another and then another. So it goes on, each subsequent village drawing ever greater gasps of awe from the casual visitor bewitched by the apparently endless spectacle of ancient charm and rustic beauty.

Then there are the fairy-tale castles and grand chateaux. The region is awash with the mediaeval giants. They sprout from every hilltop, cling to cliffs and majestically dominate the landscape. Their grandeur is breath-taking.

Yet, when these centuries old bastions, and the towns and villages surrounding them, were constructed it was for reasons far removed from that of being pleasing to your present day eye.

The crude dwellings of the general populace of the time were built out of *necessity*. People needed a roof over their heads, pure and simple. They built their hovels with whatever materials were available locally or which could easily be scavenged. There was no such thing as planning, architects drawings or building warrants. They built where they could … usually cheek by jowl with all the other peasants' shacks. Those cramped, ramshackle clusters

189

became today's quaint and charming hamlets which tourists so admire.

The castles and chateaux of the wealthy lords and barons were, on the other hand, built for a *purpose*. That purpose was defence. The constant wars and disputes of the time demanded that they inhabit a stronghold able to withstand attack and sieges of many months duration. Plus, an impressive fortress reminded the local serfs and others just where the wealth and power lay!

Thus the beauty of the mediaeval Perigord architecture which is so much admired and enjoyed by so many was born from simple necessity on the part of some and from a sense of purpose on the part of others. There was no grand artistic intent. The visual spectacle you marvel at today is but an unintended by-product of their labours.

Today, those same forces, necessity and purpose, drive much of what you do and hence shape who you are. You however, can choose, rather than leaving it to chance, to add *beauty* into your life too.

This can be applied in the physical, material and architectural aspects of your life - it is inevitably enriching to be surrounded by aesthetically pleasing things and objects. Choosing beautiful and tranquil natural settings in which to live, work and play is also spiritually uplifting.

The even more important aspect of 'putting beauty in your life' relates to the people in your life, your relationships and how you behave towards others. The key is to first set out to put beauty into the lives of others.

POWER POINT - *"Choose to put beauty in your life by putting beauty into the lives of others."*

Do this through being joyful, kind, generous, charitable, supportive and loving. Surround yourself with positive, entertaining, uplifting and like-minded people. Make time to enjoy the true beauty of life with them and through them.

Only when you achieve a balanced harmony of necessities and of purpose *and* of beauty in your life will you be able to function properly, thrive and prosper.

Consider the daily tasks and mundane chores of your life as the necessary acts, the necessities, to which you must tend regardless. Have also a purpose in your life, a greater goal (professional, personal or leisure) for which you strive. Without such a target you simply stagnate, wither and die.

And make the creation and the embracing of beauty - natural, man-made, physical and spiritual – your over-riding lifetime pursuit. Then your life will become like those country roads in south-west France. There'll be bumps and pot-holes yes, the necessities of life … but blossoming around the sweep of each bend will be golden vistas of heart-wrenching beauty, each one more stunning than the previous. Daily scenes of laughter, love, fun and compassion that you yourself will have constructed through your life of kindness and consideration to others.

Build your life like those roads, villages and castles. Build from necessity, build for a purpose … but build it to be beautiful too!

100 POWER POINTS

The Power Points highlighted throughout this publication form rules or mottoes to be followed determinedly and to live your life by. As such they are critical to your personal development. Read them, memorise them, employ them. You'll be the better for it.

This section is a reminder, a quick reference to my top 100 Power Points. No apology for the repetition!

1. "Whatever you do in life you will do it better by being cheerful and kind."

   2. "Never under-estimate the power of laughter nor the influence of the comic in society, culture and history."

3. "Concentrate only on the positives in people, see the humour and joy in every situation and find ways to help others."

   4. "Whatever you want from life, the best way to get it is to focus your energy in helping others."

5. "If you want higher self-esteem then find ways to boost someone else's self-esteem."

   6. "If you want to raise your positive spirit then assist someone else to raise theirs."

7. "If you want more happiness in life the smartest way to get it is to help someone else achieve it."

8. "Make good humour central to your personality, make a smile your calling card, spread joy and fun where-ever you go ... and laugh your way to a better, richer life!"

9. " How you perceive yourself is how others will perceive you."

10. "Ask for what you want!"

11. "Ask stupid questions!"

12. "Life may deal you a seemingly bum hand but it's how you play the hand that counts."

13. "Pick your fights carefully and strike first."

14. "When you exercise your body, you exercise your mind and vice versa."

15. "There is nothing that you do in life which you won't do better by being physically fit."

16. "There is nothing that you do in life which you won't do better by reading a book."

17. "Simple activities carried out repetitively and well are what mount up to great achievements."

18. "Live life in the present and, whatever the circumstance, always be the very best that you can be."

19. "Rise to life's challenge, choose honour and respect."

20. "A kindness given will always be returned when you most need it 'though often from a different source than to where originally gifted."

21. "There are few things in life more important than to know your angels."

22. "With humility comes compassion and inner joy ."

23. "Whatever your situation it is always possible to pull yourself up, reach for the stars and achieve the impossible."

24. "You become what you dream. So dream well!"

25. "Dare to day-dream - imagine the impossible!"

26. "The secret of life is ... to live happily!"

27. "Dreams are the spring of ambition, the source of aspiration and the font of inspiration. Dies he slowly who does not dream."

28. "Make your purpose to do things to make people happy and feel good about themselves."

29. "When faced with being right or being kind, choosing kind means that you'll always be right!"

30. "Being alone isn't necessarily a bad thing. You need to recognise the good which solitude can do to create ease within yourself."

31. "Attract into your life only joyous situations and kind people who you wish to have there."

32. "The route to certain failure is to try to please everyone. Aim only to earn their respect."

33. "It's your choice alone as to whether you enjoy a happy life or a miserable one."

34. "Live life, laugh and love!"

35. "Everyone knows deep inside themselves what is right and what is wrong – that includes you!"

36. "Honour your own right to privacy and respect the right to privacy of others."

37. "Your goal is to be a better you today than you were yesterday."

38. "Be truthful, honest, act with integrity and express with absolute clarity all that you say and do."

39. "Be ruthless in kicking out all negative influences from your life."

40. "Learning to be inwardly calm and in tune with your spiritual self is an essential part of becoming a better person."

41. "Concentration exercise should be part of your lifetime daily routine."

42. "Find mantras to which you can relate and which will fire up your drive, energy and power for the day."

43. "Work on improving your powers of concentration and watch your performances at work and at play get better and better every day!"

44. "Determination, drive and hard work are the most important building blocks to success. There is no substitute for perseverance."

45. "When you take full control of your situation and assume full responsibility for all of your thoughts and actions, success at

whatever you choose to do becomes a virtual certainty."

46. "Seek opportunity in ways to assist others to overcome adversity."

47. "Many very assured people have learned to consciously tap into and use the power of their subconscious."

48. "Learning to use your subconscious brain power expands infinitely the volume of activity with which you can cope and your ability to reprogramme your core convictions."

49. "Be the best you that you can be by being calm, relaxed and at ease with life."

50. "How do you retire an active imagination? Why would you stop doing that thing in life which you most enjoy?"

51. "Every day, in every way, I'm getting better and better."

52. "Nurture and delight your inner being by serving others needs and helping them to be the best that they can be."

53. "You cannot be a whole person nor live a perfect day without doing something for someone who will never be able to repay you."

54. "Choose to put beauty in your life by putting beauty into the lives of others."

55. "Leading a good life is about enjoying the journey!"

56. "Being in a situation is the normal state of being!"

57. "The first place that personally responsible people look when questioning events affecting them is … in the mirror!"

58. "Find those less fortunate than yourself to help and to give of your time to."

59. "Do the right thing for other people and life will do the right thing for you."

60. "Look to what exceptional people are doing – be a contrarian."

61. "Expressing yourself with simple clarity and self assurance will earn you the respect and trust of others."

62. "Only when you believe what you say will others believe you."

63. "Giving attention to others is the rarest and purest form of generosity."

64. "Those who mind about what you say don't matter and those who matter won't mind."

65. "There are no negative or positive emotions, only positivity or negativity in the way that you deal with them."

66. "Negative thoughts become negative words become negative actions. Eradicate from your brain all reference to them."

67. "Choose to dwell only on positives and you'll create a happy world all around you."

68. "Practice instant gratitude."

69. "Be clean both inside and out."

70. "Neither look up to the rich nor down on the poor."

71. "Lose, if need be, without squealing."

72. "Win without bragging."

73. "Always be considerate to everyone but particularly so to the weak and under-privileged."

74. "Be too brave to lie."

75. "Be too generous to cheat."

76. "Take your share of the world and let others take theirs."

77. "Our purpose and our duty in life is to enjoy what we do, love others and to celebrate the joy of life. Embracing these is what leads to contentment and infinite inner wealth."

78. "Act with integrity, courage, kindness and humour and others will recognise your strength and afford you respect."

79. "Your duty to yourself and to those who matter in your life is to cherish every moment of life and spend it wisely."

80. "Look for value in all that you do and circumstances where you are helping others."

81. "Put your time and energy into the daily provision of kindness and charity to others."

82. "The power of money is in having it, not spending it."

83. "Debt-free is the road to a carefree life; debt-burdened is the route to ruin."

84. "Make spiritual wealth the bedrock, and physical well-being the cornerstone, of your existence. Their healthy function guarantees success in whatever you do."

85. "The sure route to both spiritual and material wealth is the road of helping others – pure and simple."

86. "Take responsibility for your own actions and put yourself in control of your own life."

87. "Speak up for yourself ... and then always be true to your word!"

88. "A care free life is there for the taking. Just do it!"

89. "Life is as rich, enjoyable and rewarding as it should be when it is tackled head on with a positive, happy and zestful attitude."

90. "Integrate humour into every minute and everything that you do."

91. "Regardless of wealth you can only wear one shirt at a time!"

92. "The common bond that unites all successful beings is the quality of perseverance."

93. "In adversity you can find motivation. In the example of others you can find inspiration."

94. "You'll learn more from one day of failure than you will from one year of success."

95. "There's risk of some kind involved in everything you do in life, whether you like it or not. So better like it!"

96. "The only risk involved when you set out to self-improve, is the risk of becoming a better person!"

97. "The secret of success is ... to live happily!"

98. "All success flows from first becoming a better person."

99. "It is only with the heart that we see clearly. That which is essential is invisible to the eye."

100. "How far you go in life will depend on your being tender with the young, sympathetic with the striving, tolerant of the weak, respectful of the strong and compassionate with the aged. And have fun with all of them! Because some day in life you will have been all of these."

RESOURCES

Literature

Family Secrets – *John Bradshaw*

Homecoming – *John Bradshaw*

In Tune With The Infinite – *Ralph Waldo Trine*

Joseph and His Coat of Many Colours – *The Bible, Genesis*

Mastering the Art of Making Money – *Joseph T.Riach*

The Collected Works of Agatha Christie – *Agatha Christie*

The Collected Works of Carl Jung – *Carl Jung*

The Complete Psychological Works of Sigmund Freud – *Sigmund Freud*

The Instant Millionaire – *Mark Fisher*

The Man Who Mistook His Wife For A Hat – *Oliver Sacks*

The Secret World Of Self-Employment – *Joseph T.Riach*

The Simplest Sales Strategy – *Joseph T.Riach*

Too Early For A Glass Of Wine? - *Joseph T.Riach*

The Works of Lord Byron – *Lord Byron*

Winning Big In Life And Business – *Joseph T.Riach*

Online

Author's Web Site – https://www.tomriach.com . *Information on all books. Readers' reviews of his work. Press releases.*

Entertainment and Films

"A Wee Deoch-an-Doris", "I love a Lassie" and "Roamin' in the Gloamin" – *Songs written and performed by Sir Harry Lauder*

"Chariots of Fire" – *Film, producer David Puttnam, Writer Colin Welland, Director Hugh Hudson. Academy Award Best Film 1981*

"Green Green Grass of Home" – *Song written by Claude 'Curly' Putman jnr. in 1964*

"The Great Dictator" – *Film, written, directed, produced, scored by and starring Charlie Chaplin. Nominated for five Academy Awards 1940*

Quotes

"Every day in every way I'm getting better and better." - *Emile Coué*

"Fortune favours the brave … " - *Virgil (70-19 bc)*

"If at first you don't succeed ... try, try, try again" - *William E.Hickson (often erroneously attributed to Robert the Bruce, King of Scotland 1306-1329)*

"Keep right on to the end of the road … " - *Sir Harry Lauder*

"Let others wait and wonder … " - *anon*

"Nothing in the world can take the place of persistence … " - *Ray Kroc*

"Pick Yourself Up .. Start All Over Again" – *Dorothy Fields (music by Jerome Kern)*

"Possession is nine points of the law … " - *origin in old Scots law*

"Speak up for yourself … and then always be true to your word" - *my mother*

"Time and tide wait for no man … " - *Geoffrey Chaucer*

"This is no time to make new enemies ..." - *Voltaire*

"Today I'm going to take them all on and I'm going to run them off their feet! … " - *Colin Welland*

"Today I will run like the wind. Let the world watch in awe and wonder! … " - *Colin Welland*

"What the heck do they know ..." - *American comedian anon*

Sources of Inspiration

Peter Adamson – Scottish engineer and businessman

George Allen – *Childhood rival*

Harry Barclay – *Scottish farmer and entrepreneur*

Seve Ballesteros – *Professional golfer*

Richard Branson – *Millionaire entrepreneur and adventurer*

Carlos Burle – *Extreme surfer*

Andrew Carnegie – *Steel magnate, industrialist and philanthropist*

George Washington Carver – *Botanist and inventor*

Charles Chaplin – *Film actor, director and comic genius*

Agatha Christie - *Author*

Tom Cruise – *Hollywood film star*

Erna Dewachter – *Gardener, independent thinker*

Walt Disney – *Cartoonist and film maker*

Henry Ford – *Automobile manufacturer*

The Road To Joyful Living!

Maya Gabeira – *Extreme surfer*

Ann Gilmour – *Marine biologist*

Linda Grant – Orange prize winning novelist

Steve Jobs – *Founder of Apple Inc.*

Harry Lauder (Sir) – *Entertainer and comedian*

Edward Lear – *Painter and poet known for his absurd wit*

Ralph Lauren – *Fashion designer*

Garret McNamara – *Extreme surfer*

Chic Murray – *Scottish comic genius*

Iain Reid – *Real estate consultant*

Duncan Robertson – *Investment professional*

Christiano Ronaldo – *Professional footballer*

Theodore Roosevelt – *President of the U.S.A. (1901-1909)*

J.K.Rowling - *Author*

The Beatles – *Worldwide success phenomenon*

Leonardo da Vinci – *Universal genius*

Samuel Walton – *Retailer*

Valerie Weir – Childhood sweetheart

Oprah Winfrey – *Television presenter, often ranked as the world's richest woman*

Other References

Aberdeen – *Scottish city and birth place of the author*

Aberdeen Grammar School – *One of oldest schools in UK, founded 1257*

Algarve – *Most southerly region of Portugal*

Amazon – *Online retailer*

Atlantic Ocean – *Second largest of the world's oceans*

Arcachon – *Seaside resort near Bordeaux, France*

Bandol Rosé – *Wine from south of France*

Bugatti – *Automobile manufacturer (the Veyron model is the world's fastest production car).*

Cambridge – *University city in England*

Ray Ban – *Manufacturer of sun glasses*

The Road To Joyful Living!

De Beers – *World's leading diamond company*

Edinburgh – *Capital city of Scotland*

Disque Bleu – *Brand of French cigarette*

Emperor's new clothes – *The Hans Christian Andersen tale*

Fernando's tin shack restaurant – *Beach restaurant, Monte Gordo, Portugal*

Georgian New Town – *Central area in Edinburgh, Scotland*

Gitanes Brune – *Brand of French cigarette*

Iowa State Agricultural College – *University in Ames U.S.A.*

Joséphine (de Beauharnais) – *First wife of Napoléon Bonaparte*

Languedoc – *Wine region in south of France*

Mercedes Benz – *Automobile manufacturer*

Missouri – *State of the U.S.A.*

Mona Lisa – *Portrait painting by Leonardo da Vinci*

Napoléon Bonaparte – *Emperor of France 1804-1814*

Nazaré – *Town on Portugal's west coast*

Scottish Presbyterianism – *Form of protestant religion dating from sixteenth century Scotland*

Smith and Wesson .45 ACP – Popular hand gunJohn Smith's – *Popular English beer*

Sugarloaf Mountain – *A peak in Rio de Janeiro, Brazil*

Tuskegee Institute – *University in Alabama U.S.A.*

Wake Up – *The author's leisure and learning breaks, personal mentoring and business guidance courses which he conducts in the sunny south of Portugal. See https://www.tomriach.com/wakeup*